Dealing with Feeling

An Emotional Literacy Curriculum

Written and Illustrated
by
Tina Rae

"to be angry with the right person,
to the right degree,
at the right time, for the right purpose,
and in the right way."
Aristotle

Lucky Duck is more than a publishing house and training agency. George Robinson and Barbara Maines founded the company in the 1980's when they worked together as a head and psychologist developing innovative strategies to support challenging students.

They have an international reputation for their work on bullying, self-esteem, emotional literacy and many other subjects of interest to the world of education.

George and Barbara have set up a regular news-spot on the website. Twice yearly these items will be printed as a newsletter. If you would like to go on the mailing list to receive this then please contact us:

Lucky Duck Publishing Ltd. 3 Thorndale Mews, Clifton, Bristol, BS8 2HX, UK

Phone: 0044 (0)117 973 2881   e-mail newsletter@luckyduck.co.uk
Fax: 044 (0)117 973 1707   website www.luckyduck.co.uk

ISBN 1 873942 32 X

Lucky Duck Publishing Ltd
3 Thorndale Mews, Clifton, Bristol, BS8 2HX, UK

www.luckyduck.co.uk

Printed by Antony Rowe Limited

Acknowledgements

1998 has seen the emergence of curriculum materials, working parties, articles and discussion about the emotional curriculum from the "EBD" cupboard into the daylight of the classroom.

This is largely a result of two influences:

♦ The popularity of the book "Emotional Intelligence" by Daniel Goleman,
♦ The concern about the underachievement of boys for whom emotional development might conflict with macho-competitive style.

Lucky Duck Publishing welcomes this development and is pleased to include a number of new publications related to the subject. It does not feel new to us and a study of our work since 1988 will indicate that the focus of all our materials has been on interventions which encourage empathic, altruistic and self-determining behaviours from young people. For this we gratefully acknowledge the influence and work of Thomas Gordon.

Tina Rae works as an EBD support teacher and has used her illustrating talents to produce this series of lessons about feelings. She wishes to credit the influence of Daniel Goleman and also to acknowledge that she was inspired after watching a teacher deliver a lesson from the PATHS curriculum, (Greenberg and Kusche 1993)

All these resources and other materials from our publications list are referenced in the Bibliography.

Barbara Maines and George Robinson
Lucky Duck Publishing

Contents

Lessons 1 - 20

1. Feeling angry
2. Feeling sad
3. Feeling afraid
4. Feeling happy
5. Feeling surprised
6. Feeling loved
7. Feeling shocked
8. Feeling bored
9. Feeling jealous
10. Feeling ashamed
11. Feeling lonely
12. Feeling greedy
13. Feeling nervous
14. Feeling disappointed
15. Feeling rejected
16. Feeling shy
17. Feeling arrogant
18. Feeling generous
19. Feeling selfish
20. Feeling intimidated.

Appendix 1   More Resources
   • a cover for a feelings book
   • some blank illustrated pages
   • a problem solve worksheet
   • 32 problems to solve - ideas for follow up work.

Introduction and Background

This programme is designed to be used with all pupils in the Primary Phase since, at certain times in their school careers, every individual will probably experience some difficulty in managing his/her behaviour and emotions. These difficulties, often associated with changes in both the home and school context, will be exhibited in a variety of ways and for some pupils the difficulties experienced will be pronounced enough to merit the differentiation of the schools behaviour management programme which enlists the support of parents, staff and other agencies and usually includes work on raising self esteem and developing more positive relationships with peers and adults.

However, much recent research has shown that all pupils need and will benefit from becoming emotionally literate and in developing adequate social and emotional skills, in order to be able to modify their own behaviour. (Greenberg and Kusche 1993, Elias and Calbby 1992). Schools have a clear focus and a required commitment to teaching the curriculum and basic skills, i.e. the three 'Rs'. It is becoming increasingly evident, however, that without a further commitment to teaching the fourth 'R' i.e. life and social skills of problem solving, empathy, cooperation and emotional literacy, schools will be failing many pupils. Without these skills and the sense of personal identity, self esteem and self control that can result from focusing upon them, some pupils will also not develop the academic and basic literacy skills they require in order to reach their full potential.

The understanding of feelings and emotions is central to any programme which aims to teach this fourth 'R'. In order to become emotionally literate children "need to become aware of feelings in order that their own and other's feelings might in turn be acknowledged, managed, accepted and thought about" (Paul Greenhalgh 1996). This was also acknowledged in the National Curriculum Councils (1989) Curriculum Guidance 2 - Curriculum for All.

Writers such as Rutter (1991) suggest that schools can help children to manage the stress and difficulties encountered in their own lives:

> "it is not high school achievement that seems to make a difference, rather, it is positive experiences of a kind that are pleasurable and rewarding and which help children develop a sense of their own worth together with the confidence that they can cope with life's challenges and control what happens to them." (p. 8)

A Preventative Approach

This programme aims to provide teachers with a preventative programme - to enable pupils to develop the skills they need. Alongside teaching the 'academic' curriculum, many primary teachers have frequently made use of circle time approaches to aid in developing and promoting a school values system, and in teaching manners and appropriate behaviour. This programme aims to focus further on feelings and emotions more specifically.

The focus is on emotional and social skills which can aid children in developing awareness of themselves and others and in managing their own behaviour and emotions more effectively. Naturally, there can also be a positive enhancement of their ability to learn in the school context.

The Oxford English Dictionary defines emotion as "any agitation or disturbance of mind, feeling, passion; any vehement or excited state". Daniel Goleman's (1995) definition adds clarification:

> "I take emotion to refer to a feeling and its distinctive thoughts, psychological and biological states, and range of propensities to act". (p 289).

There are obviously hundreds of emotions and a continuing debate as to how they can or should be grouped/classified. The idea that there are a few 'core emotions' is supported by Paul Ekman's work, (1994), at the University of California at San Francisco. He found that specific facial expressions for fear, anger, sadness and enjoyment were recognised by people from cultures all around the world. These are considered to be universal emotions.

For the purposes of this programme, which is aimed at developing emotional awareness in children in the Primary phase, I will classify emotions and then develop a series of activities around them. The main categories as set out by Daniel Goleman are as follows:

- Anger
- Sadness
- Fear
- Enjoyment
- Love
- Surprise
- Disgust
- Shame

Clearly, within such categories there will be mention of the 'related family' of emotions, i.e. for Anger we will also focus upon fury, and irritability and the jealousy that may be felt prior to/alongside such anger. Each emotion will be introduced, generalised and reinforced via a series of lessons. These lessons will generally include:

1. Introducing the emotion
2. Providing examples of situations which might engender such a feeling (usually via stories)
3. Discussion - the children will talk about times they have felt such an emotion
4. Role play - in order to experience emotions in safety and learn to empathise with others
5. Practical and recorded activities and suggestions for follow on work
6. Teaching self control strategies where appropriate
7. A reinforcement time.

These lessons are designed to meet the following objectives:

- ◆ to enable pupils to identify and gain a deeper understanding of the feelings we all regularly experience
- ◆ to develop an emotional vocabulary
- ◆ to further increase empathy for others and awareness of how personal feelings and behaviours can impact upon others
- ◆ to develop a range of self-control strategies and encourage pupils to express anger appropriately - without fighting
- ◆ to encourage pupils to be reflective and to understand consequences
- ◆ to improve pupils self-concept.

Individual Education Plans (IEPs)

This programme can form the basis of a whole class or small group project and be used flexibly in order to meet individual needs and requirements, aiding in the formulation of Individual Education Plans for certain pupils. Targets relating to feelings can be made specific and linked to the objectives listed. Pupils can be encouraged to become involved in setting their own targets and monitoring their own progress in this area. This involvement is clearly crucial as:

"There is positive association between pupil's involvement and greater motivation and feelings of self-worth on their part. Pupils should be encouraged and guided in setting and organising learning goals according to their age and understanding; monitoring their own progress; reflecting on their learning, personal and social situations; describing their preferred tasks and work areas; and working cooperatively with their peers" (Circular 9/94 DFE 1994 para 31).

Tracking Changes - Success Criteria

It is important that the target class, group or individual pupils who have been identified and begun this Emotional Awareness Training programme, are carefully monitored. This may involve more regular review meetings or evaluation sessions and a more systematic approach to re-defining and forming specific targets. I am certain that there is no 'magic wand' or 'formula' in this approach. However, if the general concept of training children to become emotionally literate is seriously understood and consistently incorporated into the curriculum of the school as a whole, then I am sure that positive, measurable outcomes will result. One such outcome, in some American schools who have included emotional literacy in their curriculum, has been a significant drop in the number of suspensions. (Goleman - p 283).

Changes and developments can be tracked via references to the 'success list' and teachers, parents and children can review progress with reference to this list. This could also then highlight areas for revisiting; reinforcement and future focus/targets.

The Success List

- ♦ improved recognition and naming of own emotions (vocabulary)
- ♦ more understanding of causes of feelings and behaviours
- ♦ improved management of anger
- ♦ improvement in self esteem/self-concept - more positive feelings regarding self
- ♦ fewer fights and verbal attacks on others
- ♦ improved self control
- ♦ improved listening skills
- ♦ improved performance in class work
- ♦ improved understanding of others feelings, i.e. empathy
- ♦ improved understanding of how actions and behaviour can affect others (consequences)
- ♦ more able to listen to others
- ♦ more understanding of relationships
- ♦ more able to share and take turns
- ♦ improved skills for solving conflicts.

A Personal Note

This programme has been developed and made use of with individual pupils, small groups and whole classes in Primary schools. It has been, and continues to be, further developed and refined but does, at present, provide a clear structure and starting point for teachers alongside building upon the use of circle time (Bliss and Tetley 1993, Bliss et al. 1995) in the Primary phase. Teachers in schools can and will further develop and extend the lessons, making them more appropriate for their own groups of children and classes.

It is hoped that the supporting philosophy and intentions of this programme are clear. Being emotionally aware means having essential life skills which, in turn, lead to more fulfilment and success. Emotional Awareness Training may, hopefully, begin to foster such skills.

"While not every boy and girl will acquire these skills with equal sureness, to the degree they do, we are all the better for it."

(p 285) Goleman 1995

The Structure of the Programme

The programme is divided into 20 sections and each section focuses upon a specific feeling, providing a complete lesson and ideas for reinforcement and follow-on work.

The lessons are arranged in the following sequence

1. Feeling angry
2. Feeling sad
3. Feeling afraid
4. Feeling happy
5. Feeling surprised
6. Feeling loved
7. Feeling shocked
8. Feeling bored
9. Feeling jealous
10. Feeling ashamed
11. Feeling lonely
12. Feeling greedy
13. Feeling nervous
14. Feeling disappointed
15. Feeling rejected
16. Feeling shy
17. Feeling arrogant
18. Feeling generous
19. Feeling selfish
20. Feeling intimidated.

The Structure of the Lessons

Each lesson is structured to a six (or seven*) point plan:

Activities	Objectives
Definition	to introduce and identify the feeling
Story	to help pupils recognise, understand and discuss the feeling as experienced by people in the story
	to encourage and further develop listening skills
Questions for Discussion	to encourage reflection and understanding of consequences
	to encourage listening and turn taking skills
	to increase pupils' understanding and recognition of how their feelings and behaviours can impact upon others, i.e. empathy.
Role Play	to encourage pupils to recognise the emotions of others
	to encourage cooperation skills
	to generalise and reinforce the emotion in a safe way - i.e. they are 'acting' and therefore not being 'themselves'.
Activities	to generalise and reinforce the feeling
	to promote cooperation and listening skills.

*An extra section - Self Control Strategies is used for some feelings which might lead to negative or hostile behaviours.

Self Control Strategies	to introduce a specific method in order to promote behavioural skills
	to encourage pupils to use an 'inner dialogue', i.e. self-talk
	to encourage pupils to make use of a stepped approach to problem solving.
Reinforcement	to encourage pupils to develop their own 'control' strategies and methods
	to encourage pupils to become more reflective.

Notes for Teachers - How to use the Programme

The lessons can be followed in sequence as they begin with a focus on the most commonly understood and experienced feelings, e.g. anger, sadness, and then move on to more sophisticated feelings, e.g. arrogance, rejection and pride etc. They can be adapted for use with individual pupils and used directly with small groups and whole classes.

Definition

The definition aims to introduce and identify the feeling/or to label the feeling. The definition given at the start of each section can be written up onto the blackboard or whiteboard by the teacher prior to the start of the session. It is preferable to make use of a portable whiteboard for this part of the lesson or the photocopiable format given in each lesson plan, as this can be the focus of the initial whole class 'brainstorming' or discussion session. A circle and brainstorming approach can be used in order to encourage pupils to offer their own definitions or ideas and the teacher can act as a scribe for the pupils or nominate a pupil to take on this task, so as to produce a list of definitions.

It is important to encourage the pupils to develop their own definitions for the feeling as this clearly aids understanding and clarifies meaning on a personal/individual level. However, as with circle time approaches, no pupil should be required to make such a contribution - ideas need to be volunteered.

The Story

A story which highlights and focuses upon the defined feeling then follows. This aims to help pupils recognise, understand and discuss the feeling as experienced by the characters in the story. The story also aims to focus on encouraging and developing listening skills.

The story should be read to the individual, group or class by the teacher. At all times, it will be necessary to read with real expression and sincerity - you must be convincing.

It is important that the story is read by the teacher in order to ensure that pupils are really focused and listening and that they understand that this is their contribution to the process.

Questions for Discussion

At the end of the story there is a series of questions which clearly test pupils' comprehension but also encourage pupils to reflect, think about consequences, develop an understanding and recognition of how their feelings and behaviours can affect others, and to highlight the differences between positive and negative relationships. The questions should be asked by the teacher who also needs to ensure that contributions are made by all pupils who are willing - if possible! As this is again like the definition part of the lesson, an oral activity, I would suggest that the pupils should remain seated in some type of circle arrangement. It is also important that 'appropriate' and 'right' answers are reinforced by the class teacher.

The central character in most of the stories tends to 'do the wrong thing' at some point in the narrative and one of the questions for discussion usually highlights this and asks what he/she 'should' have done for the best or what they could now do in order to rectify the situation. It is extremely important to allocate adequate time for responses to this kind of question as this type of problem solving activity is usually central to the next part of the lesson.

Role Play

The role play/drama activity takes place after the questions for discussion. From experience of teaching the programme, this section of the lesson has proved to be the most enjoyable part for the majority of pupils as it provides for a 'safe' way to generalise and reinforce the feeling, i.e. the pupils are required to act the parts of characters in the story and are not required to be themselves. These activities encourage the pupils to interpret others' feelings and views. Most of the role play activities require the pupils to work in groups of 5/6 and to 'act out' a better ending to the story and then to perform their scene to the rest of the class. This is clearly a fun and exciting part of the lesson for most pupils but requires careful management by the teacher, e.g. pupils need to be placed into appropriate groups and these groups should be organised by the teacher in order to ensure, as far as possible, a sensible 'mix' of ability, gender and friendship groups. These groups can remain static or can change on a weekly basis - depending on the general make-up of the class. It is also important to allocate sufficient time for the groups to negotiate and agree on the content of their scenes and to practise prior to performance!

The classroom will need to be arranged so as to allow for 4/5 groups to have a working space and then to provide an 'audience' and 'performing' space. This is not difficult, i.e. move the furniture to the sides of the room or to one end of the room, but this probably needs to be done prior to the start of the lesson itself.

The teacher needs to facilitate the groups via constant movement around the room to 'visit' each one in turn and to prompt and reinforce the appropriate story lines and problem solving approaches.

It would be wise to reinforce some 'ground rules' prior to the start of each session, alongside clarifying what is actually the expected outcome. These could be as follows:

♦ everyone in the group needs to think of ideas and solutions
♦ everyone needs to use their imagination
♦ everyone must be careful not to criticise others' ideas
♦ everyone will try to improve and build upon each others ideas until all agree the structure and content of the scene.

Remember that some pupils may have more difficulty than others in taking part in such an activity and it is essential that this is handled with sensitivity and care.

Activities

After each role play/drama session, ideas are given for follow-on activities which aim to generalise and reinforce the feeling alongside prompting cooperative working practices and listening skills.

Clearly, there will not always be adequate time to complete all the suggested activities and the teacher may well want to choose one activity or allow pupils to choose one activity from the suggested list.

Another option would be to photocopy the Activity Worksheet for the feeling and present this to the pupils as the set activity for the lesson. Each lesson has such a supporting worksheet which usually involve pupils engaging in a recorded activity, e.g. acrostic-poetry, writing a 'better ending', cartoons, drawing, etc.

These worksheets or activities can be presented in A4 folders or home-made project books in order to ensure that a special record is kept of individual pupil's work in the programme. A suggested photocopiable format for a Feelings' book is provided in the programme but pupils may prefer to design their own book/ folder covers for these special books/files. (This can be found in the appendix).

Self Control Strategy (This element is not included in every session.)

On completion of one of the set activities or the Activity Worksheet, the next part of the session involves making use of the self control strategy. This specific traffic light method is aimed at promoting behavioural skills, and encourages pupils to conduct an inner dialogue, make use of a stepped approach to solving problems and to attempt to control certain impulses. (This method is developed from the one described in Daniel Goleman's book p276).

When the lesson presents pupils with a specific problem relating to a negative feeling, (e.g. anger - someone is saying bad things about your mum in the playground), the pupil is presented with a structure which involves taking the following steps:

- ◆ stop and calm down — recognise that this is the time to use the self control strategy

- ◆ think before acting — define the problem and the feelings

- ◆ set a positive goal — think of as many solutions as you can

- ◆ take action — try out your best plan.

It is preferable for pupils to work on solving the feelings problems in small groups or with a partner, and for the 'ground rules' made use of in the role play activity to be reinforced.

The teacher will need to reinforce this stepped approach at the start of this part of each session and may want to enlarge the traffic light method format to A3 size for this purpose.

Pupils can then be presented with the problem and record their responses at each of the steps on the traffic light method worksheet provided. The responses can be recorded in short notes so as to take away the pressure of writing at this stage in the lesson. A pupil's response to the 'angry' problem might then be recorded, as on the example overleaf.

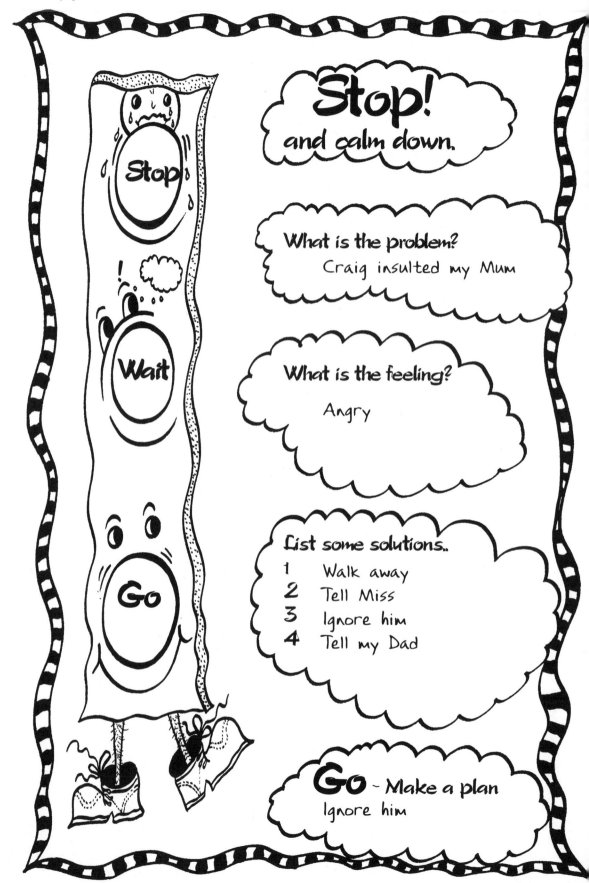

Reinforcement

This final activity aims to further support pupils in developing their own 'control' strategies, encouraging them to become more self aware and reflective. This takes the form of a Reinforcement Worksheet which can be completed by the individual pupil at the end of the lesson and presented in his/her folder or special feeling book. It is important that, if required, this activity is a 'private' one. Some pupils may want to share their personal experiences and ways of coping whilst others may not at this stage. The teacher needs to emphasise that this is a personal record and that the main aim of completing the task is for the individual pupil to gain a personal insight into his/her own feelings and to develop or think about how this specific feeling affects them and whether or not they can develop appropriate self control strategies to deal with the particular feeling as and when appropriate.

A particular emphasis in this activity is placed upon enabling pupils to discriminate between 'comfortable' and 'uncomfortable' feelings. It is important to note that feelings are not labelled 'good' or 'bad' - after all it is clearly 'good' to be angry if someone is making racist statements even though the feeling may not be a comfortable one at the time in question. Also - it may be good to feel fear in certain situations if it induces you to run from a dangerous situation. This particular point like many others which will arise out of discussions and activities in these lessons, will no doubt require sensitive handling by the teacher but will certainly ensure that there is not a dull moment during the implementation of the programme!

Bibliography

Bliss T. and Tetley, J., (1993) Circle Time. Lucky Duck Publishing.

Bliss, T., Robinson, G. & Maines, B., (1995) Developing Circle Time. Lucky Duck Publishing.

Cam P. (ed) (1993) Thinking Stories: Philosophical Inquiry for Children, Hale & Ironmonger.

Coles, M.J. & Robinson, W.D. (1991) Teaching Thinking, London Duckworth.

Curry, M. & Bromfield, C. (1994) Personal and Social Education for Primary Schools Through Circle Time. NASEN.

DFE Circular 9/94 1994 para. 31. Pupils with Problems.

Elias, M. J. and Clabby, J., (1992) Building Social Problem Solving Skills: Guidelines from a school based programme, Josey-Bass.

Ekman P. (1992) 'An Argument for Basic Emotions" in Cognition and Emotion, 6, p. 169-200.

Ekman, P. & Davidson, eds. (1994) 'Fundamental Questions About Emotions' New York: Oxford University Press.

Fisher R. (1996) Stories for Thinking Oxford Nash Pollock.

Foot, H.C. Chapman, A,J. and Smith J.R. (eds) (1980) Friendship and Social Relations in Children. New York Academic Press.

Greenberg, M.T. and Kusche, C.A. (1993) Promoting Social and Emotional Development in Deaf Children. The PATH programme. Seattle. University of California Press.

Greenhalgh, P., (1996) Behaviour: Roles, responsibilities and referrals in the shadow of the Code of Practice. Support for Learning Vol 11 N0 1.

Goleman, D. (1995) Emotional Intelligence Why it can matter more than I.Q. London, Bloomsbury.

National Curriculum Councils (1989) Curriculum Guidance 2 - Curriculum for all.

Newton C, Wilson, D and Taylor, G (1996) A Circle of Friends in Educational Psychology in Practice Vol. 11, No 4.

Rutter, M. (1991) Pathways from Children to Adult Life. Pastoral Care in Education. Vol. 9 No. 3.

Schroeder A. (1996) Socially Speaking Cambs. L.D.A.

Spence, S. (1980) Social Skills Training with Children and Adolescents: A Counsellor's Manual. Windsor NFER.

Lesson 1

Feeling Angry

Definition
is not always comfortable
and you feel like hitting out.

Story I - Angry

Pam went into the playground with Caris. They were really excited because it was the first time they'd been allowed to play with the new games ordered by their teacher last term. All the children had been asked what sort of things they'd like to have to play with at break-times.

It was amazing - they had discussed it for what seemed like weeks, made lists and given them to the teacher. Finally, all the new equipment had arrived. Miss Jones had shown it to them in assembly. It looked brilliant - skittles, soft ball, swing bats - lots of great games. Every class was to have a turn each week to try something new. Year 5 could have the American bowling equipment today. Everyone was really excited. Miss Jones had helped them to sort out teams.

"You're in my team," said Pam.

"I know," said Caris. "I bet we win."

The two girls went to collect the balls while other children from Year 5 set out the skittles. Each child was allowed to have two turns and then the team leaders had to total up the number of skittles they'd knocked over between them. It was quite hard to hit the skittles at first but it seemed to get easier as they went along.

"I love it," said Caris - even though she'd missed all the skittles the first time.

"I'm sure we'll all get better with practise," said Miss Jones. She was smiling.

"Look at John!" shouted Pam. "He's knocked over all eight in one go - brilliant".

John walked to the back of the line and stood behind Caris.

"That was good." she said.

"You were rubbish!" he said. "If you don't get better we'll lose this game."

Caris went red.

"Don't be like that," said Pam. "Caris was trying her best. We can't all be as good as you."

"Who asked you fatso?" said John and he punched Pam hard in the back.

 ## Stop

Caris didn't think. She just suddenly got angry - really angry. Her face was red. All of a sudden her heart seemed to be beating really fast. Before John could move away or say anything else, she grabbed his head, pulled it down and kicked his face.

"Stop! Stop!" shouted Pam.

But it was too late .... the blood was everywhere.

Questions for Discussion

1. What made Caris so angry?

2. Was she right to be angry?

3. Why was John angry?

4. Is it important to win? Why?

5. What do you think will happen next?

6. Have you ever felt angry like this? When? Why? What happened?

Act the Story

Act out the story until you get to the STOP face.
Try to make up a different ending which is happy.

Activity

Write your own ending to the story from the STOP face. You may want to use the computer and work with a friend. You can make up a mini book and illustrate it.

Stop Light
Use the traffic light method to solve the problem - someone keeps cussing your mum when you go in the playground.

Read the letter from Alex and discuss with a partner.

What is the problem?
What could Alex do?

When you think that you have some good ideas, write him a reply.

What other feelings might Caris and Pam have had when John insulted and hurt them?

Reinforcement

Complete the reinforcement worksheet.

Stop!
and calm down.

What is the problem?

What is the feeling?

List some solutions..
1
2
3
4

Go - Make a plan

AN ANGRY LETTER

Dear Student,

Please help me. I feel so angry. Every day when I go to school I get into a fight or an argument at play time. People say just one bad thing to me and I feel like hitting them. I get into trouble with the teacher and she says 'why are you so horrid to everyone and so angry?' I don't know but I know I need some help. What can I do to stop myself from hitting out? How can I get some friends? Can you help me?

Please write back. Yours, Alec.

Can you help Alec? What would you suggest? Write back - work with a friend.

Dear Alec,

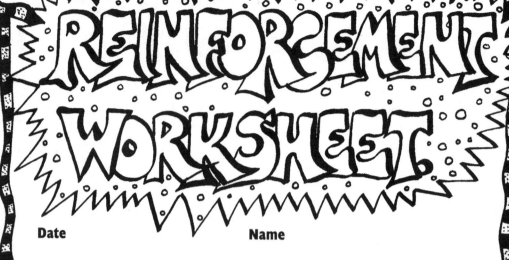

REINFORCEMENT WORKSHEET

Date

Name

When do I feel angry?

How does it feel?

Is it a comfortable or uncomfortable feeling?

What does it make me feel like doing?

Do I need to help myself when I feel like this? If so, how can I?

If I need help, who else can help me?

This is me when I am angry.

Lesson 2

Feeling Sad

Definition
is when you feel unhappy
and full of sorrow
and want to cry.

Story 2 - Sad

Hal went down to the kitchen. It was very early - too early to get up really but he was wide awake.

"I can't stay in bed any longer," he thought. "I'll go down and get a drink and put on breakfast TV."

He crept down the stairs as he didn't want to wake his mum. Last night had been horrible. They'd had another argument and this time dad had said he was going. He couldn't stand it any more - that's what he'd said.

But what was it that he couldn't stand? Hal wasn't sure. He knew his mum wasn't happy - they both had rows almost every day. Then, last night, dad had said he was going and mum had been crying. He could hear it through the bedroom walls.

He sat down and sipped his cup of tea and flicked channels to get the Cartoon Network. It was his favourite and normally he laughed out loud - but not today.

Slowly the door creaked open - it was his mum.

"How are you? Do you want some breakfast?"

"Yeah - thanks mum," he said.

"Are you okay though?" she asked again.

He looked at her.

She looked so tired and all red around the eyes.

He tried to say something but he couldn't. It seemed there was a big lump stuck in his throat.

"Please don't cry," said his mum.

Hal bit his lip but he couldn't help it - tears were trickling down his face. He got up and ran to the bathroom, locking the door behind him.

Questions for Discussion

1 Why had the last night been 'horrible' for Hal?

2 Why do you think he didn't laugh at the cartoons?

3 What do you think Hal wanted to say to his mum?

4 What do you think will happen next in this story?

5 Do you think Hal will be able to feel happy in the future?

6 Have you ever felt sad like this? When? Why? What happened?

7 Were you able to stop yourself feeling sad or did you have to wait for the feeling to gradually go away?

Act the Story

Act the story until you get to the STOP face.

Try to work out how Hal can tell his mum how he is feeling and what she will say to him. Your ending may be sad or happy.

Activities

Discuss in groups or as a whole class some times when children might feel sad.

Sometimes people feel sad for a long time and sometimes for just a short time. Sometimes we can stop ourselves feeling sad and other times we have to wait for a while before we can stop this feeling.

Think of two times you were sad - one for a short time, one for a longer time.

For example:

Short term sadness
My friend didn't want to play with me.

Long term sadness
My Gran died and I really miss her.

Write about these two kinds of sad feelings - think of one short term and one long term sadness you have felt. How did you feel? How did you cope or deal with it? What did you do? Who helped you? Does the sadness still come back sometimes? Use the activity sheet.

Stop Light
You feel really sad about the way your mum and dad keep fighting. When your mum asks you if everything is OK you say nothing.

Use the traffic light method to solve the problem.

Reinforcement

Finally, complete the Reinforcement Worksheet for Sadness.

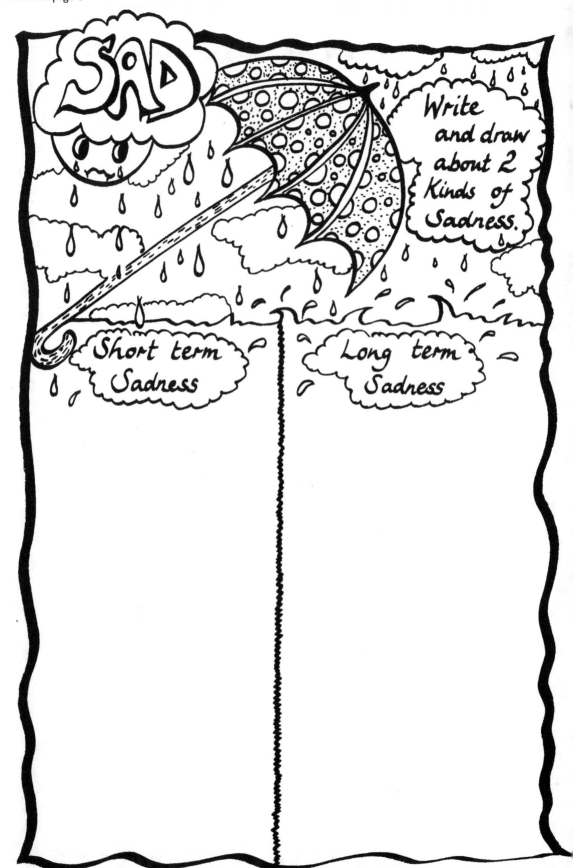

Write and draw about 2 Kinds of Sadness.

Short term Sadness

Long term Sadness

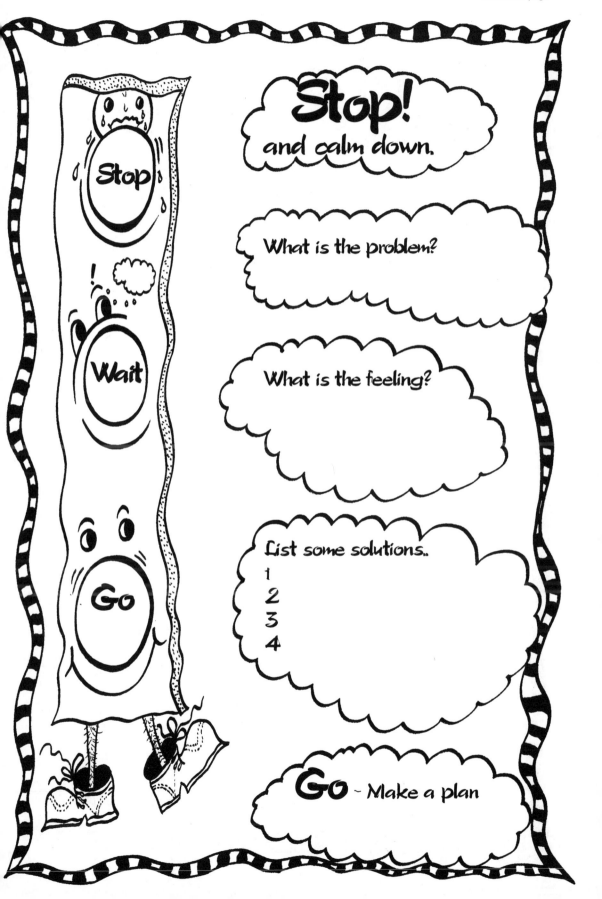

REINFORCEMENT WORKSHEET

Date   Name

When do I feel sad?

How does it feel?

Is it a comfortable or uncomfortable feeling?

What does it make me feel like doing?

Do I need to help myself when I feel like this? If so, how can I?

If I need help, who else can help me?

This is me when I am sad.

Lesson 3

Feeling Afraid

Definition

is when you feel alarmed and scared
of someone or something.
Your heart may beat fast and you may
want to run away.

Story 3 - Afraid

Jake was really looking forward to Friday night because his two friends were coming round and staying over. They'd planned it for what seemed like weeks.

"We'll have a midnight feast," said Sam.

And watch the late night movie," said Raff.

Raff loved scary films - he was always writing horror stories in Free Writing lessons - much to the annoyance of Miss Best, their class teacher.

"I don't know why she doesn't like them," said Jake.

"Too much blood and gore for her I expect," said Raff. "You know what girls are like."

"Yeah - soft in the head," said Sam.

When Friday finally arrived the boys were really excited. Sam's mum dropped him off just after 6 o'clock and Raff came round with his aunty at ten past.

"Be good," they said as they went off in the car.

"Of course we will," retorted the boys.

They loved coming to Jake's house as his mum was such good fun - she always got a take-away and let them have anything they wanted from the fridge.

But tonight she said she felt really tired.

"I think I've got a migraine coming," she said. "So I'll just go to bed - you will be okay boys, won't you? And don't go up to bed too late, okay?"

Okay," said the boys.

"Great," said Jake. "we can watch the horror movie now."

The film was brilliant - all about a mad axe murderer who terrorised a group of kids on a summer camp. The boys watched transfixed as they ate the remains of the pizzas. It finished at 1.00am.

"We'd better creep up ..... mum would kill me if she thought I'd stayed up this late," said Jake.

They tiptoed to the door. Then they suddenly heard a scratching sound. It grew louder and louder and faster and faster as they moved towards the door.

"Oh my god," said Sam. "What the hell is it?"

The boys stood frozen. Jake felt sick.

"It's the axe murderer," whispered Raff. "He's come to get us .... he's going to get us right now .... aaaah!"

He fainted just as the door burst open with a great bang.

"I'm coming to get you," said a deep voice.

"Run for it!" shouted Sam - but it was too late! They were trapped!

Questions for Discussion

1   Why do you think Raff likes scary films so much?

2   Why did the boys think Jake's mum was 'good fun'?

3   Why would Jake's mum be angry if she knew that they'd stayed up so late?

4   Would she be angry because they'd watched the scary film?

5   Why did the boys become so scared?

6   What do you think will happen next?

7   Have you every felt really frightened or scared like this? When? Why? What happened?

Act the Story

Act the story and make up your own ending. Who is going to be at the door? You can make the ending scary, funny or sad.

Activities

Use the worksheet to make an illustrated list of "things that make me afraid" .

Talk to a friend about your list and notice whether you have chosen different things.

Think about why these things scare you.

How can you help yourself to overcome these fears?

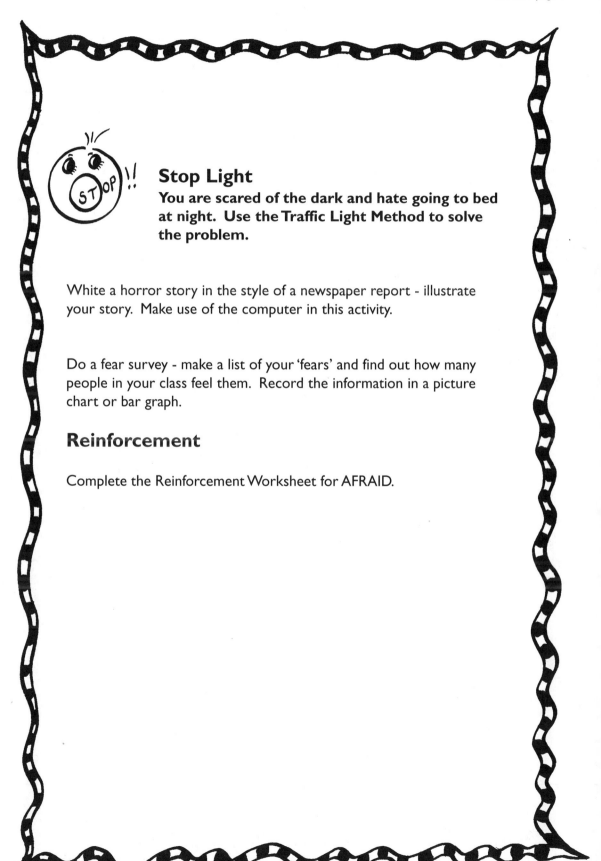

Stop Light
You are scared of the dark and hate going to bed at night. Use the Traffic Light Method to solve the problem.

White a horror story in the style of a newspaper report - illustrate your story. Make use of the computer in this activity.

Do a fear survey - make a list of your 'fears' and find out how many people in your class feel them. Record the information in a picture chart or bar graph.

Reinforcement

Complete the Reinforcement Worksheet for AFRAID.

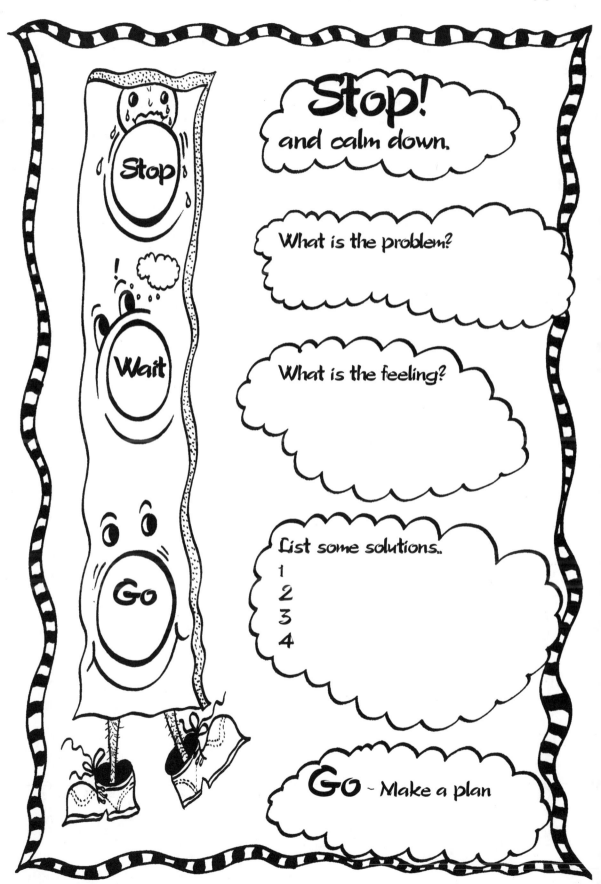

REINFORCEMENT WORKSHEET

Date   **Name**

When do I feel afraid?

How does it feel?

Is it a comfortable or uncomfortable feeling?

What does it make me feel like doing?

Do I need to help myself when I feel like this? If so, how can I?

If I need help, who else can help me?

This is me when I am afraid.

Lesson 4

Feeling Happy

Definition

is when you are enjoying yourself
and want to smile.
It's a warm and comfortable feeling.

Story 4

It was Basil's birthday. He was ten. When he woke up that morning he felt really great - a lovely, warm feeling - not like last year when his mum and dad had split up. It was funny ... everyone had said to him that he'd stop feeling sad about it all. He hadn't believed them at the time but he did now.

He jumped out of bed and ran straight into the living room.

"Happy Birthday Basil," said his mum. She kissed him on the cheek and gave him a small box.

"Go on! Open it then!"

He pulled off the paper. It was a portable CD player.

"Oh thanks mum - that's really brilliant! Just what I wanted."

Mum smiled. "Now get ready quickly because dad's coming to fetch you in half an hour."

"Okay mum."

Basil's dad picked him up at 10 o'clock.

"Happy Birthday Basil," He smiled. "I haven't got you a present yet. Well, at least - it's not here. We've got a journey first of all."

That's why Basil loved his dad - he never did boring things. They were always unusual.

Basil laughed.

"Come on then!"

He jumped into the car. His mum got in too.

"I didn't think you were coming as well mum," said Basil.

"Well, I am young man! Your dad and I have finally come to an agreement. We might not want to be married to each other but we can still be friends and be a family," said Mum.

"Yeah - and that means all of us getting together on your Birthday, Basil" said his dad.

Basil bit his lip.

"It's funny," he thought. "I feel so happy I could cry," - but he didn't.

"Where are we going then?" he asked.

"Ha ha!" said his dad. "Just you wait and see."

"We'll give you one clue though," said his mum. "You'll need a passport and a cowboy hat."

"I don't believe it," shouted Basil.

"You'd better!" replied his dad.

Questions for Discussion

1   Why did Basil feel so happy when he woke up?

2   What had he felt like on his last birthday?

3   What did Basil like so much about his dad?

4   What did Basil's mum mean when she said "We can still be a family"?

5   What do you think will happen next? Where will they go?

6   Have you ever felt so happy or enjoyed yourself so much you thought you could cry? When? Why? What happened?

Act the Story

Act out Basil's brilliant day. Think of all the good fun and funny things that might happen and what would be the end to a perfect day.

Activities

Make a 'happiness is....' book.

List all the things that make you happy and either draw them or find pictures from a magazine to stick into the book.

Draw cartoon pictures to make a Happiness Poster. Use speech bubbles and get your friends to fill in what the character is saying.

People can feel happy and enjoy themselves if they feel good about themselves. Write a list entitled:

10 ways to cheer up a friend

or

10 ways to stay happy

Work in groups and share your ideas.

Write a happy poem. Make an ACROSTIC. Use one of these words:

ENJOYMENT
PLEASURE
HAPPY

for example

Happiness is
Always meeting kind
People who give
Pleasure and make
You smile.

Reinforcement

Complete the reinforcement Worksheet for HAPPINESS.

HAPPINESS

REINFORCEMENT WORKSHEET

Date   **Name**

When do I feel happy?

How does it feel?

Is it a comfortable or uncomfortable feeling?

What does it make me feel like doing?

Do I need to help myself when I feel like this?

How can I help other people when I feel happy?

This is me when I am happy

Lesson 5

Feeling Surprised

Definition

is when you feel very excited by something sudden or unexpected. It can be comfortable or uncomfortable or maybe even both at the same time.

Story 5 - Surprised

Jason ran down the street as fast as he could possibly run. He didn't know why but he just felt like he needed to do something - anything - just to stop himself getting any more upset. As he turned the corner he bumped into his friend Alex.

"Ow!" said Alex. "Watch where you're going will you." He suddenly stopped. "Oh, it's you Jason. You were going so fast that I didn't even see you. How's everything going?"

"Okay .... you know," said Jason.

"Oh no, Isn't it you birthday today .... I've just remembered - Happy Birthday Jas .... I'm so sorry .... I forgot."

Jason went red. "Oh, it's okay .... "

"Sorry," said Alex again.

"Well, it's okay really .... it's just that .... well, everyone seems to have forgotten. I don't know what's happening really .... "

"What do you mean?" asked Alex looking puzzled.

Jason looked away. Alex could see that he was quite upset. Then he understood.

"Oh no - you mean .... your mum and dad and everyone .... they've all forgotten!" said Alex in total disbelief. Jason nodded.

"But they can't have done .... maybe .... well, they're just playing a trick or something."

"No, honestly - I know them. They wouldn't do anything like that. It's not the sort of thing they'd do. I know my mum and dad have just forgotten. I looked at the calendar on the fridge door. That's where mum writes all the birthdays, doctor's appointments, term dates .... stuff like that - and there was absolutely nothing on it today."

"Nothing?"

"No - nothing. I only looked because usually - in fact, every year on my birthday mum comes upstairs with a present and cards. She didn't even get me up on time today. I can't believe it."

"That's why you've been funny all day in school" said Alex. "Look .... come on, I'll come to your house now .... you'll have to say something to your mum. It might be easier if I'm with you."

Jason gave him a weak smile. "Thanks mate," he said.

As the two boys turned the corner they heard music coming from one of the houses.

"That's my favourite track," said Jason.

"I know," said Alex as they reached his house.

At that moment Jason's mum and dad ran out through the front door with all his friends behind them. It was just like a sea of blurred faces to Jason. Everyone was laughing, shouting "Happy Birthday!" and throwing party poppers in the air. Jason was so surprised that he just stood motionless with his mouth open. His face was bright pink.

"B...b...but... I thought ...." he began.

"We know," said his mum. "You thought we'd forgotten, but we hadn't."

"We just wanted to do something really special," said his dad. "Especially as it's your last year at Junior School - we wanted to surprise you."

"Well you've certainly done that," laughed Jason. He turned to Alex "And you .... you knew all along, didn't you?"

Alex laughed out loud. "Honestly, your face was a picture!"

"Come on," said his dad. "Let's go in and enjoy it."

And that's exactly what they did!

Questions for Discussion

1   Why did Jason 'need' to run so fast?

2   What had Alex forgotten?

3   Do you think Jason meant it when he said "Its okay"?

4   How did Jason know that his mum and dad had really forgotten? Can you give two reasons?

5   Did he have any idea at all that his mum and dad would organise such a party?

6   Have you ever had a lovely surprise? When? What happened?

Act the Story

Try to show how surprised Jason felt when he got to his house. Think about how he would look and what his voice would sound like.

.

Activities

Use the worksheet to write your own story called 'The Surprise'. Try to think of as many different words to describe this feeling.

Design and make up a special surprise for someone you know and like. Try to think of what they would really like and what would surprise them. Record this on the surprise card. Illustrate your card!

Sometimes we get a 'pleasant' surprise and it makes us feel happy and comfortable. At other times the surprise might be 'unpleasant' and cause feelings that are sad and uncomfortable. Work with a partner and make two lists and see if you agree which surprises are 'pleasant' or 'unpleasant'.

Work in a group of 4 - 5. Use a felt tip and a large sheet of paper to record your writing. Make a list of words which mean almost the same as surprised. There are some ideas at the bottom of the page. You can use a dictionary or a thesaurus.

Reinforcement

Complete the Reinforcement Worksheet for SURPRISED.

amazed, astounded, shocked.

REINFORCEMENT WORKSHEET

Date   Name

When do I feel surprised?

How does it feel?

Is it a comfortable or uncomfortable feeling?

What does it make me feel like doing?

Do I need to help myself when I feel like this? If so, how can I?

If I need help, who else can help me?

This is me when I am surprised.

Lesson 6

Feeling Loved

Definition
A special feeling when you know you are cared for and accepted.. someone has a real affection for you.

Story 6 - Feeling Loved

Cara ran out of the house and into the back garden. She looked back at the windows with their curtains blowing out in the breeze. She felt so happy - she thought she'd burst. She ran to the old shed at the end of the garden and sat on the grass with her head resting against the door.

I don't believe it, she thought to herself. That morning Pam and John had said they were going to adopt her. So, for the first time in eleven years she was going to have a real mum and dad - just like other children in her school. She had been living with them since she was eight but always thought that she'd be moved on again at some point. She smiled again and suddenly realised that she had tears running down her cheeks.

Just them she saw Sally jump over the fence between their two houses. She ran up to Cara.

"Are you okay Cara .... what's wrong?" she asked.

"N...n...nothing's wrong - its .... it's all fine ...."

"But why are you crying?"

"It's just .... I'm so happy," said Cara, and she burst into tears.

Sally put her arm around her friend and cuddled her.

"Come on .... whatever it is .... it can't be that bad ... Come on, I'll help if I can."

"It's okay," said Cara, between whimpers. She took a deep breath and wiped her face with the back of her hand. Then she turned to her friend.

"I'm not sad - honestly. In fact, I'm really happy. It's just that .... well, I've never felt like this before and I needed to come out here and sort myself out."

Sally looked puzzled.

"I don't understand," she said.

"Well - it's just .... all these years I've lived with lots of families since my mum got really ill."

Sally nodded, "I know."

"And this is the first one that I've felt really okay with and .... well .... happy. You know .... Pam and John are so kind and they've made me feel like .... well .... like they love me ... "

"But they do Cara - you must know that. You're just like a real daughter to them - they always wanted you, accepted you and wanted you to be happy."

"That's exactly it," said Cara. "They want me to be a real daughter. They've got the papers through and they're going to adopt me - like, they'll be my real mum and dad."

Sally jumped up and pulled Cara with her.

"That's brilliant," she shouted and hugged her friend really tightly.

"I'm so glad - I know you'll be my friend for life. Oh Cara - it's great!"

Cara smiled. She'd stopped crying.

"I know. It's just, I couldn't cope with it. When they told me, I had to run out of the house. They said they really loved me and wanted me to be with them for always. I just went all pink. I couldn't handle it so I ran out."

"Oh Cara, come on. Let's go in together," said Sally. "You need to tell them how happy you are and how much you love them too."

Cara took a deep breath.

"I'll try," she said as the two girls walked back into the house.

Questions for Discussion

1   Why did Cara feel so happy?

2   Why did she cry when she was so happy?

3   Did Sally think that Cara was happy or sad? Why?

4   What had happened to Cara once her mum had become very ill?

5   Why was Sally so pleased with Cara's news?

6   What did Cara feel when Pam and John had said they would adopt her? Why do you think she said "I couldn't handle it"?

7   Why do you think Cara might find it difficult to show her feelings and tell Pam and John how much she loves them too? Do you think she had felt rejected in the past? Why?

8   Who do you think loves you like this? How do they show this love to you? How does being loved make you feel?

9   Who do you love in this way? How do you show this feeling to others? Do you find it easy or difficult to show that you feel love for someone?

Act the Story

You need to act this story in pairs. If you want you can change the names of the characters to suit the make up of your group, e.g. Cara and Sam, Bob and Alex, etc. Try to really show all the different feelings that Cara experiences in this short space of time.

Activities

Finish the story. Write your own version of the story and your own ending. Think carefully about the conversation that Cara will have with Pam and John.

> How will she explain why she ran out of the house?
> How will she tell them that she loves them and feels so happy that they want her to stay with them?
> What will they all do to celebrate? Think of a treat!

Compose a class LOVE IS book. Each member of the class to make up one sentence and illustrate this for the book; e.g.

Love is... caring for your friend.

Love is... making dinner for your mum when she feels ill.

Love is... helping your sister with her reading.

You can use the writing frame for this.

Design a collage picture about someone you love and use balloons or cloud labels to show what you love about that person. Use the picture frame on worksheet 7.

Reinforcement

Complete the Reinforcement Worksheet for feeling LOVED.

Someone I love

REINFORCEMENT WORKSHEET

Date **Name**

When do I feel loved?

How does it feel?

Is it a comfortable or uncomfortable feeling?

What does it make me feel like doing?

Do I need to help myself when I feel like this?

How can I help other people when I feel like this.

This is me when I am loved.

Lesson 7

Feeling Shocked

Definition

Feeling shocked is when you feel so surprised that you may become virtually immobile and even unable to speak.

Story 7 - Shocked

It was Saturday night and Jake was really excited. His two friends were coming to stay and mum had promised them a video, a pizza and three games on the lottery. Of course, they weren't allowed to go and get the tickets themselves, but mum would let them pick their own numbers and then go to the corner shop and put them on. At first he had laughed at this mum when she'd watched the lottery on telly but it was almost as if he'd caught her bug. When it came on he got just as excited as her - even through he knew the odds were ridiculous.

"It must be one in a trillion chance that we'll win," he said to his mum.

She agreed - "But I just can't help it - it keeps me going even to think I might have such a minuscule chance."

That night the boys had a game of football in the local park until it got too dark to see properly.

"Come on," said Sid. "It's getting cold."

"And I'm hungry," said Eddie.

The boys ran down the road and got back to Jake's house in record time. All the boys were out of breath as they stood in the doorway. They rang the bell but there was no answer.

"What's going on?" said Jake. "Mum should be there."

"What's the time?" said Eddie, trying to catch his breath.

"It's 8.15," said Sid. Then he nearly jumped - "8.15!"

"Oh no," said Jake. "We're over an hour late - I told mum we'd be back by seven - she'll kill me," he gasped.

"Well, she would if she was in - I don't understand this Jake - your mum didn't say she was going out did she?"

"No of course not - the last thing she'd do is go out and miss them calling the numbers."

"Well come on," said Eddie. "Let's look round the back - maybe she's in the kitchen getting a drink of something."

The boys ran down the side of the house and peered in through the kitchen window. They stood transfixed with their mouths open as they saw Jake's mum. She was standing in the middle of the room, bolt up-right, not moving at all and just staring at the kitchen table.

"She looks like a statue," said Sid. "What on earth's wrong?"

"I don't know - but I'm going to find out," said Jake. He went in.

"Mum ... mum ... what is it? Are you okay?" he shouted. His mum didn't move. Agnes from next door came into the kitchen clutching a bottle.

"It's okay boys," she said laughing. "Don't worry - your mum's just in shock - that's all." She sat Jake's mum down and poured her a drink.

"What do you mean - shock?" said Jake.

"Now just sit down - because I think this is going to be a shock to you as well." Jake looked at her. He sat down. "Your numbers in the lottery - they've all come up."

"WHAT?" screamed Jake as he fell off his chair and then stood up. He was pink in the face. He looked at his mum and then sat down again.

"I think you are all in shock," said Agnes. "I've never seen you boys so quiet in my whole life."

"No, neither have I," said Jake's mum, finally managing to speak. She laughed and gave Jake a hug. "I still can't believe it," she said.

"N....neither can I," said Jake. But they had to the next week when the mega cheque arrived - plus half the national newspapers and television stations. "How did you feel?" they asked. Jake and his mum looked and laughed. "There's only one word to describe it," she said. "Shocked!"

Questions for Discussion

1   Why was Jake so excited?

2   What does "the bug" refer to?

3   Why were the boys over an hour late?

4   How could Jake be so sure his mum hadn't gone out?

5   Why did Sid describe Jake's mum as looking like a statue?

6   Why did Agnes think Jake was 'in shock' too?

7   Have you ever had a shock? When? Why? What happened?

Act the Story

Try to show how shocked the characters were. Pay special attention to facial expressions and voice tones.

Activities

The 'Big Shock' - write a story with this title. Try to describe accurately how someone who is in shock actually looks and sounds. You can use the newspaper style sheet for this.

Imagine that some-one has had a shock/ surprise. Draw them before and after. Think about the colour of face, size of eyes, etc.

Reinforcement

Complete the Reinforcement Worksheet for SHOCKED

REINFORCEMENT WORKSHEET

Date   **Name**

When do I feel shocked?

How does it feel?

Is it a comfortable or uncomfortable feeling?

What does it make me feel like doing?

Do I need to help myself when I feel like this? If so, how can I?

If I need help, who else can help me?

This is me when I am shocked.

Lesson 8

Feeling Bored

Definitions
is when you feel fed up, tired and weary of everyone and everything. You are too restless to get excited or enjoy anything at all.

Story 8 - Bored

It was the summer holidays at last. Everyone had been looking forward to them for so long that it seemed amazing when they finally arrived. Basil was really excited. He had planned so many things to do with his friends that none of them really knew when or where to start. They'd decided to go swimming, bowling, to the Athletics Club and to the Art Club run by Miss Mills at the school.

Jake had also persuaded everyone in the gang to put up tents in his back garden. They were going to have an open air midnight feast.

I can't wait, thought Basil as he ran home. He met his mum at the gate.

"I'm just going shopping," she said. "Do you want anything?"

"No - it's okay - thanks mum."

She turned round and caught his arm. "I forgot to tell you - Jake's mum 'phoned to say that the tent party's off on Friday. Apparently, they've been offered a friend's flat in Spain so they'll be away all summer now"

"Oh no!" said Basil. He looked upset.

"Never mind," said his mum. "Sam's not going away is he? So you'll have someone to pal about with."

It won't be the same though, thought Basil. Jake's such a laugh and makes everything good fun - even boring things like walking to school.

Basil went inside the house and kicked the old cupboard. He always did that when he was angry. His mum said that it was better than kicking a person or an animal. He went upstairs feeling very fed up.

It just won't be the same without Jake, he thought. Nothing is - it'll all be boring whatever we do. The swimming will be boring and the bowling and the Art Club - as for athletics, I think I'll definitely give that a miss - it'll be the most boring of all.

He lay down on his bed and put his pillow over his face. Just then the 'phone rang. It was Jon.

"Hi Bas - the Athletics Club starts tomorrow and there's a big competition at the end of the second week with prizes and everything"

Basil grunted.

"Well - are you coming?" said Jon. He sounded really keen.

"I don't know," said Basil in a bored voice.

"What do you mean - you don't know! What's wrong with you?"

"Oh - nothing," said Basil. He spoke slowly. "It's just - I don't know."

"You don't know?" asked Jon again.

"No," grunted Basil.

"Oh come on Bas - you're the best sprinter in the school . You could easily win the 100m and it will be in the paper afterwards you know. Come on - don't be boring."

"I'm not being boring!" said Basil indignantly. "I'm just bored that's all - and I'm bored with you bothering me, so - so just don't."

He slammed the 'phone down before Jon could reply. He lay back on the bed again and stared up at the ceiling. Then he realised what he'd just done. Bored or not - he had no excuse. But it was too late now - or was it?

Questions for Discussion

1   Why was everyone so excited about the summer holidays?

2   What was it that made Jake so special?

3   Do you think that kicking the cupboard is a good way to deal with the feeling of anger?

4   Why did Jon think that Basil would definitely want to go to the Athletics Club?

5   How do you think that Basil could have helped himself to deal with his bored feeling?

6   What do you think will happen next?

7   How could Basil sort this situation out now?

8   If Jake had been in Basil's position, would he have acted in the same way? If not, why not?

Act the Story

Act the story until you get to the STOP face. Try to make a better ending for Basil. Think carefully about how someone might look and move around if they're feeling bored.

Activities

Write a good ending to the story. Think particularly about the conversation between Basil and Jon. How will Jon help Basil get out of this 'mood'?

Do a class survey - 'what bores you?'

What do you find boring?

    the news

    spelling

    sums

    washing up.

Present your work in a picture chart or bar graph.

 ## Stop Light
Use the traffic light method to solve the problem - Basil thinks nothing will be fun if his friend is away. What can he do?

Your three best friends are away for the summer holidays. How will you stop yourself from becoming bored and lonely?
Make a list of things that you could do. Use the traffic light method to work out your best plan.

Use the activity sheet to solve Barney's problem.

Reinforcement

Complete the Reinforcement Worksheet for the feeling BORED.

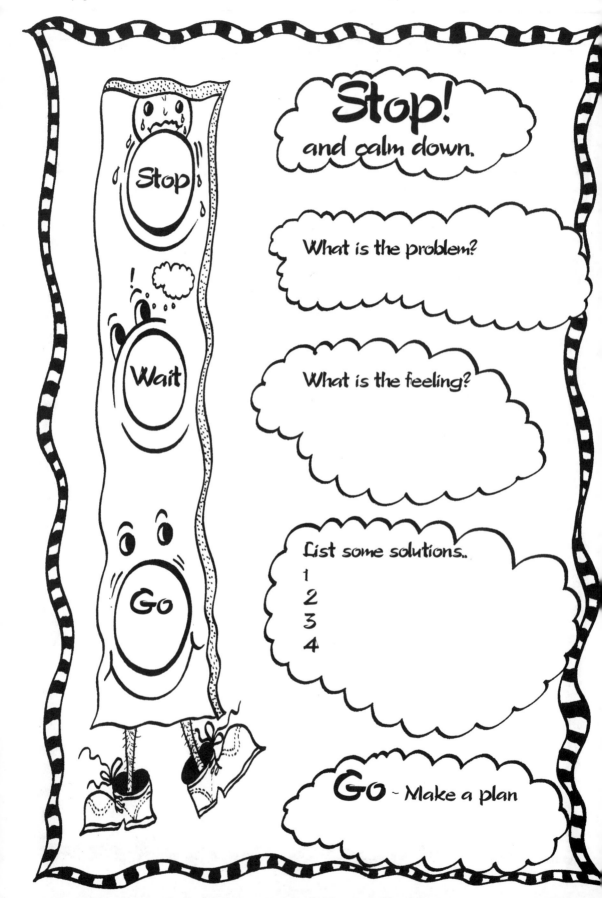

REINFORCEMENT WORKSHEET

Date **Name**

When do I feel bored?

How does it feel?

Is it a comfortable or uncomfortable feeling?

What does it make me feel like doing?

Do I need to help myself when I feel like this? If so, how can I?

If I need help, who else can help me?

This is me when I am bored.

Lesson 9

Feeling jealous

Definitions
is horrible because you want things which belong to other people.

Story 9 - Jealous

Janet woke up at 7.30am. The first thing she thought about was Alicia. "What a stupid name" she thought. She would be called something stupid like that - yes - she'd have to have a posh name - it couldn't be something ordinary like everyone else. She got out of bed and went to the bathroom. In fact she ran to the bathroom to get in before her four brothers and younger sister.

I bet she doesn't have to queue to use the toilet, she thought. Once breakfast was out of the way and mum had checked their uniforms, the five children set off for school. Janet was the oldest. She hated it. Her mum just didn't have time to give her any attention because the twins were only five.

"Go on," said mum. "You're all ready ... and mind you walk them carefully Janet and take care of your brothers."

"Yes mum," said Janet in a quiet voice.

"Are you okay? You seem a bit quiet Janet."

"Yes ... I'm fine mum," said Janet.

"No she's not," said James. "She's fed up because it's the school play next week and Alicia Painton's been picked for the star part."

"And she's got a ball gown and posh shoes," said Sam.

"Yeah - she's the prettiest in the class so she's going to be Cinderella," said Daniel. "I bet Jan will be the ugly sister!"

The boys all laughed. Janet went red. She stared down at her feet.

"Now - don't be nasty," said mum. "I'm sure the teacher will be fair."

As they walked down the road, Janet felt more and more angry. I hate her ... I really hate her, she thought. She's got everything - she's pretty, she's good at all her work and people like her - everyone does - but I don't. I can't stand her stupid posh little voice.

Just as they arrived in the playground Alicia ran straight up to Janet.

"Hi Janet - isn't it exciting - we're going to start rehearsals today - it'll be really good," she said.

"Oh shut up," said Janet.

"Oh ... I'm sorry ... are you okay Janet ... I... I haven't upset you or anything have I ... you would say ..."

"No, you've not upset me - I just can't stand your stupid whiney voice so clear off," said Janet and with that she walked away with her nose in the air.

Alicia was shocked. She didn't know what she'd done to make Janet feel like that. Perhaps it wasn't me, she thought. Perhaps she's had an argument with one of her brothers. I'll try and talk to her again later.

Janet went into the classroom. She knew she wasn't supposed to go in before the bell but she still did. She looked around to make sure no one was looking. Then she picked up a pot of the printing ink they'd been using in yesterdays Art lesson and tipped it into Alicia's tray.

That'll teach her, she thought. Then she suddenly noticed the rack of cos- tumes for the play. On the end of it was a beautiful pink dress covered in gold thread. It was Alicia's dress. She picked up a pair of scissors and started to cut right through the skirt.

Just then, the door creaked slightly. "Janet - what are you doing?"

It was Mr Malek their class teacher. He pulled the scissors from her hand. "Well - what ARE you doing?" he repeated.

Janet looked at the floor. She went red. She felt really sick - but it was too late now.

Questions for discussion

1   Why do you think Janet hated being the eldest?

2   Was it true that Janet's mum didn't give her any attention?

3   Why was Janet jealous of Alicia?

4   Why did she try to ruin Alicia's work and the dress?

5   What do you think will happen next?

6   What could Janet have done in order to stop feeling like this?

7   Have you every felt jealous of someone? When? Why? What did you do?

Act the Story

Act out the story until you get to the STOP face. Can you make up a different ending so that Janet and Alicia become friends?

Activities

Draw a picture/cut out a picture of your favourite pop star/sportsperson/film star.
What is so special about him or her?
Why do you like him or her so much?

List your thoughts around the picture.

Now think about why someone might be jealous of him or her?
Would they be 'right' to feel like this?

Use the activity sheet for your picture and your list.

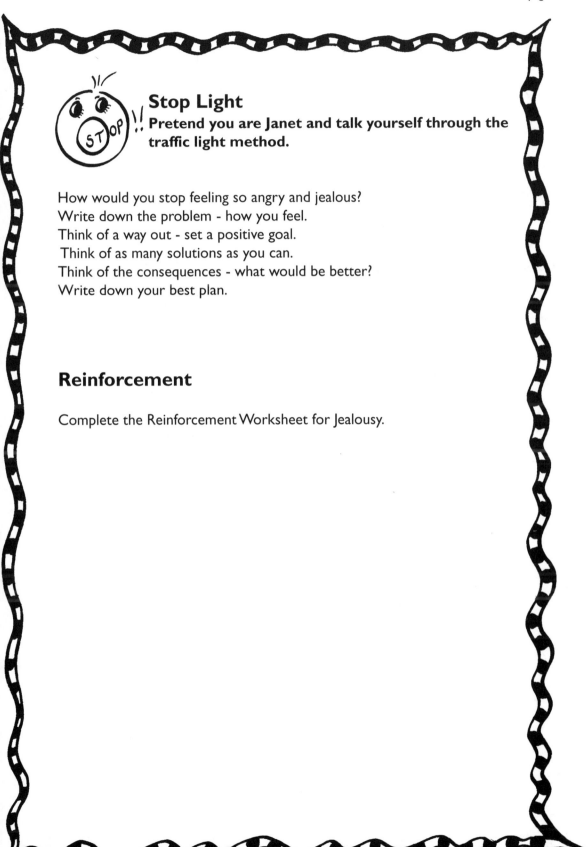

Stop Light

Pretend you are Janet and talk yourself through the traffic light method.

How would you stop feeling so angry and jealous?
Write down the problem - how you feel.
Think of a way out - set a positive goal.
Think of as many solutions as you can.
Think of the consequences - what would be better?
Write down your best plan.

Reinforcement

Complete the Reinforcement Worksheet for Jealousy.

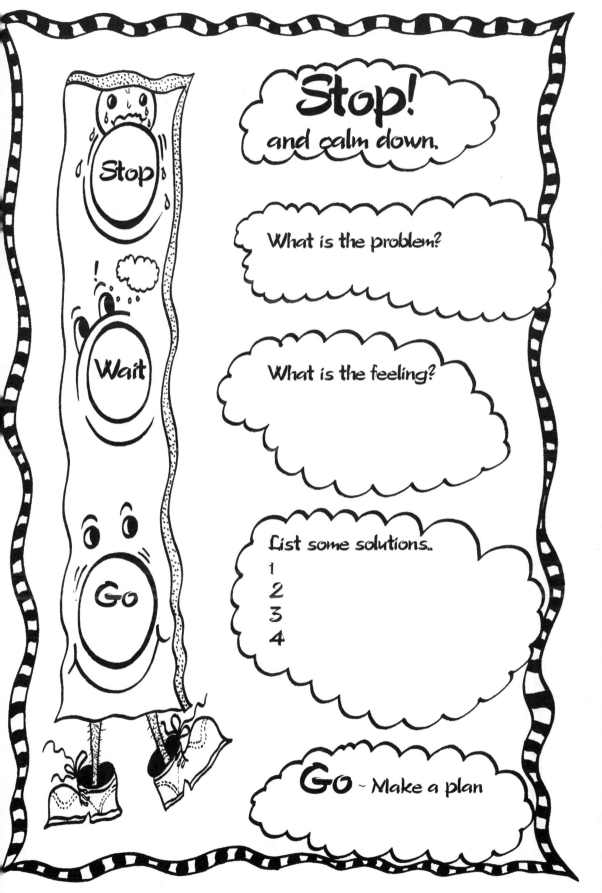

REINFORCEMENT WORKSHEET

Date   Name

When do I feel jealous?

How does it feel?

Is it a comfortable or uncomfortable feeling?

What does it make me feel like doing?

Do I need to help myself when I feel like this? If so, how can I?

If I need help, who else can help me?

This is me when I am jealous.

Lesson 10

Feeling Ashamed

Definitions

is an extremely uncomfortable
feeling you experience when you have
done something wrong or bad.
You feel disgrace and guilt.

Story 10 - Ashamed

Sara had really been looking forward to the weekend as her dad had promised to take her shopping for new trainers. The old ones were just about finished. She'd quite liked them when they were new but everyone else in her class seemed to have bought new ones and she didn't want to feel left out. People could be horrible sometimes. She remembered how Alan and Maya had teased her last Friday and said she'd looked like a tramp in her old clothes and trainers. She went red just thinking about them. Mayo had been particularly nasty -

"Look at her ... scruffy old bag! Does she really think we'd go around with her looking like that!"

Sara had just walked away and ignored them but she was really furious inside.

On Saturday morning she got up really early. She was ready before eight o'clock. At ten past eight there was a 'phone call. Her mum answered it. Sara knew that it was her dad.

"Sorry love - but your dad's had to go up to Scotland. His Aunt Ella's not very well."

Sara looked at the floor.

"Now ... don't get upset. He'll come next weekend."

"But he was going to get me trainers mum." said Sara. She felt tears prickle her eyes.

"You'll have to wait love - it's only a week." said her mum. "I'd lend you the money if I could but I need everything in my purse this week-end as we're due to do a big food shop today."

Her mum went upstairs to get ready for her own shopping trip.

Sara ate her cornflakes slowly. She felt so angry. They'll just laugh at me again next week ... I can't bear it, she thought.

Just then she noticed her mum's purse by the bread bin. She didn't stop to think. All she saw were the new trainers she wanted so much. They cost eighty pounds. She opened the purse. That was exactly what Mum had. She took the notes and quickly squashed them into her jacked pocket. She put her cereal bowl in the sink and then shouted upstairs to her mum.

"I'm just going out mum. I'm going round to Claire's house, now I know dad's not coming."

"Okay love - I'll pick you up at three o'clock when I've done the shopping," her mum replied.

Sara ran out of the house and down the road to Claire's house. She could feel the money in her pocket.

I won't tell Claire, she thought. I'll wait until Monday and surprise her with my new trainers. She decided to go and buy the trainers before going to her friend's house. Mum won't know I didn't go straight there.

Just then, she heard a car screech to a halt right by the side of the pavement. Sara jumped and looked round. It was her mum! She looked really white as she got out of the car.

"I think you've got something that belongs to me Sara."

Sara looked away. She went red. Just in that minute she realised what she'd done.

"How could you?" said her mum. She wasn't shouting.

"I feel so ashamed of you."

Sara tried to speak but she couldn't. She felt sick and ashamed but it was too late now.

Questions for discussion

1   Why did Sara think she might be 'left out'?

2   Why had Maya and Alan teased Sara? What do you think of their behaviour?

3   Why did Sara steal her mum's money?

4   What do you think Claire might have said to Sara if she knew she'd stolen the money?

5   Why do you think Sara's mum didn't shout at her?

6   What do you think will happen next?

Act the Story

Act the story in pairs until you get to the end. Try to work out a conversation between Sara and her mum. How will Sara 'put it right'? What will she say?

Activities

Write a 'good' ending to the story - from the STOP face.

Write an acrostic poem using the activity sheet.

Pretend you are Sara. Talk yourself through the problem using the Traffic Light Method. What alternatives do you have?

Think about some of the things that have caused you to feel ashamed. Fill in the questionnaire by circling the 'yes' or the 'no' if it is something you have ever been ashamed about.

You can keep this private and confidential if you do not want to show it to anyone.

Questionnaire

Taking something that belongs to someone else   yes / no

Teasing or name-calling someone   yes / no

Telling lies   yes / no

Copying someone else's work   yes / no

Dropping rubbish around the school   yes / no

Putting someone down in front of friends   yes / no

Forgetting to meet someone   yes / no

Not helping at home as much as you should   yes / no

Reinforcement

Complete the Reinforcement Worksheet for ASHAMED.

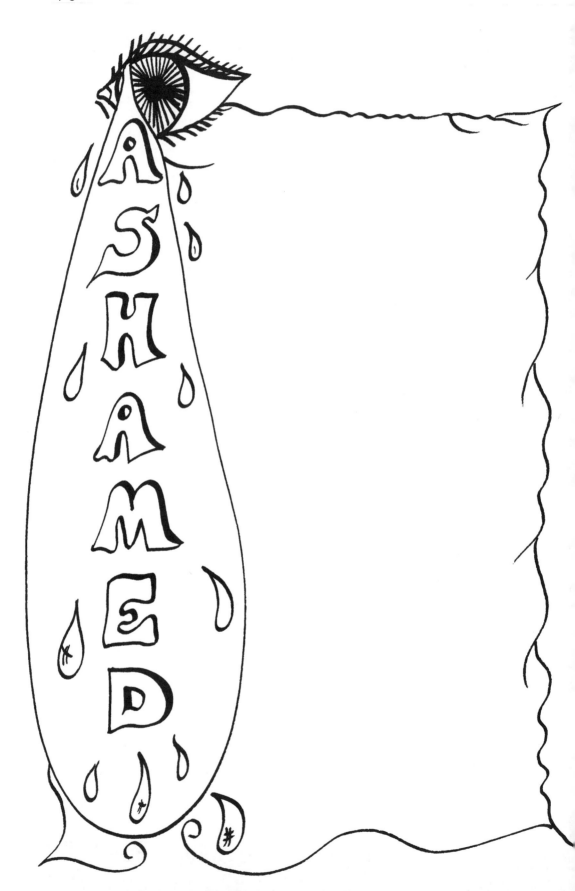

Stop! and calm down.

What is the problem?

What is the feeling?

List some solutions..
1
2
3
4

Go - Make a plan

Stop

Wait

Go

REINFORCEMENT WORKSHEET

Date   **Name**

When do I feel ashamed?

How does it feel?

Is it a comfortable or uncomfortable feeling?

What does it make me feel like doing?

Do I need to help myself when I feel like this? If so, how can I?

If I need help, who else can help me?

This is me when I am ashamed.

Lesson 11

Feeling Lonely

Definitions
is when you feel left out, on your own and not included. It is usually not a comfortable feeling.

Story 11 - Lonely

Jon was looking forward to starting his new school. There was a brilliant uniform and his mum had bought him a new bag and trainers for P.E. He was particularly looking forward to doing basketball and all the other new games which they couldn't do at the primary school - mainly because there wasn't a big gym - just a little hall which had to be used for dinners as well. Oldfields High sounded great The only problem was that none of his friends were going there. At first, it looked as though Rick and Hal might be but then they'd been offered places at a school nearer to their homes so they'd chosen that.

All the boys had been excited about starting new schools but Jon didn't feel quite the same way this morning. He couldn't explain it but he just felt a bit uneasy as he packed his lunch box into his bag.

"I wish Rick and Hal were coming with me," he thought.

Just then his mum shouted up the stairs. "Come on Jon - hurry up - you don't want to be late on your first day!"

"Okay mum, I'm just coming down," he said.

He picked up his bag and ran down the stairs.

"Well - you look really smart," said his mum as they got in the car.

The journey wasn't too bad - only about half an hour. Suddenly Jon found himself waiting at the school gates watching his mum drive off to work. He turned round. The building looked enormous. Even though he'd seen it before when they had to go and have a first look around, he couldn't remember it being this big. He looked back at the gates. There seemed to be hundreds of kids going in. Everyone was shouting and laughing. Some of the boys looked huge - taller than his Uncle Pat. Jon took a deep breath.

Well, I'd better make a move, he thought as he heard the bell. He walked into the main building where he saw a big notice board. It said:

Year 7 Students
Report to Mr. Palfreyman in Room A36

Where's A36? he thought. He looked around. There were lots of younger looking boys standing there. They all seemed to be chatting and laughing. Jon continued to stare at the board.

"They all know each other," he thought. "They must be friends from the same school." He felt his stomach turn over. "I wish that Hal and Rick were here."

He continued to watch the other boys. They all seemed to be really happy and excited. One boy was telling a story about his holidays and how he'd been allowed to ride a motorbike in Greece because they thought he looked older than he really was. Jon listened but felt as if he was on the outside - as if he was watching all the other kids on telly or something.

Just then he felt someone slap him on the back.

"Hi Jon - how's it going?"

He turned round.

"Michael! I didn't know you were coming here!" Jon shouted. Michael had been in the Year 6 gang and played in the football team with Jon.

Michael laughed, "Neither did I - until yesterday. My mum had appealed and they finally sent a letter to say I could come. It's great isn't it?"

"It sure is," said Jon. He smiled as he realised just how great it really was.

Questions for discussion

1   Why do you think that Jon was looking forward to starting his new school?

2   Why didn't he feel quite the same way on this particular morning?

3   What do you think he was actually feeling and thinking as he got ready?

4   Do you think that everyone else at the school gates really felt happy and okay?

5   Why did Jon feel his stomach turn over?

6   What difference do you think that Michael will have made to Jon?

7   Have you ever felt lonely like this? When? Why? What happened? How did you cope with this feeling?

Act the Story

Try to show the change in Jon - how lonely and worried he felt and how much better he felt once he'd met Michael. Think about how people move around if they are feeling lonely or excluded. Show the difference between how he looks when he arrives and how he looks when he has met up with Michael.

Activities

Imagine that you are starting a new school. Write a story called 'The First Day'. Show how you felt lonely at the start of the day and how, by the end of the day, you had managed to feel more like one of the crowd and been able to make new friends.

Stop Light

You want to play with your friends. You see your sister looking sad in the playground when you are in the middle of a game.

Problem solve using the Traffic Light Method. Your little sister says she feels lonely at her new school. She thinks no one wants to play were her. Go through the Traffic Light Method and devise a plan for her to deal with this problem. Write out her best plan. Work in pairs.

Write a "Loneliness is ......" poem. Try to write at least ten sentences beginning with this phrase. The whole class could brainstorm for ideas and vocabulary before you tackle this activity. These ideas might trigger your own thoughts and examples:

Loneliness is...

a sad feeling.

Loneliness is...

when others don't want to play with you.

Loneliness is...

wishing someone was there to watch your favourite cartoon and share a pizza.

Illustrate your poem.

Use the worksheet to brainstorm 5 things you can do to help Jon.

Reinforcement

Complete the reinforcement worksheet for the feeling LONELY.

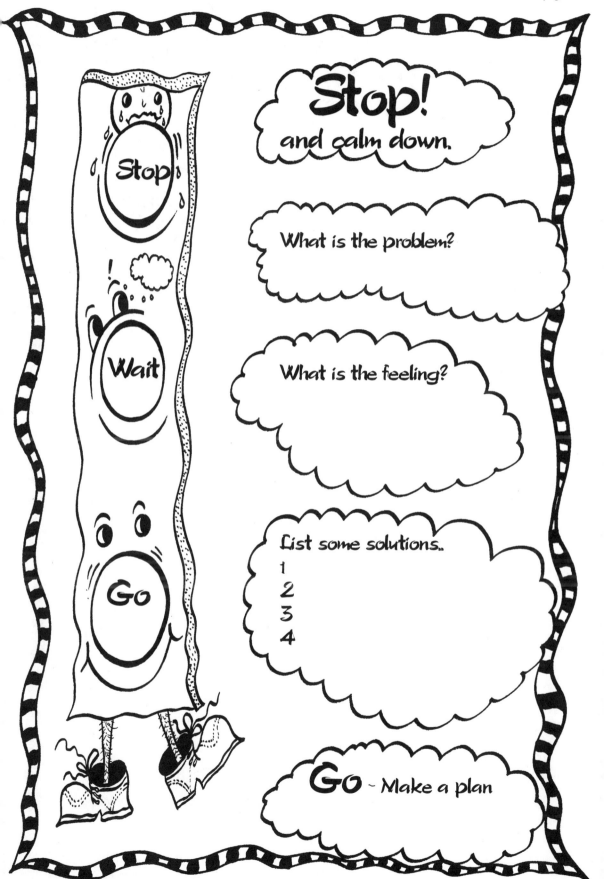

REINFORCEMENT WORKSHEET

Date **Name**

When do I feel lonely?

How does it feel?

Is it a comfortable or uncomfortable feeling?

What does it make me feel like doing?

Do I need to help myself when I feel like this? If so, how can I?

If I need help, who else can help me?

This is me when I am lonely.

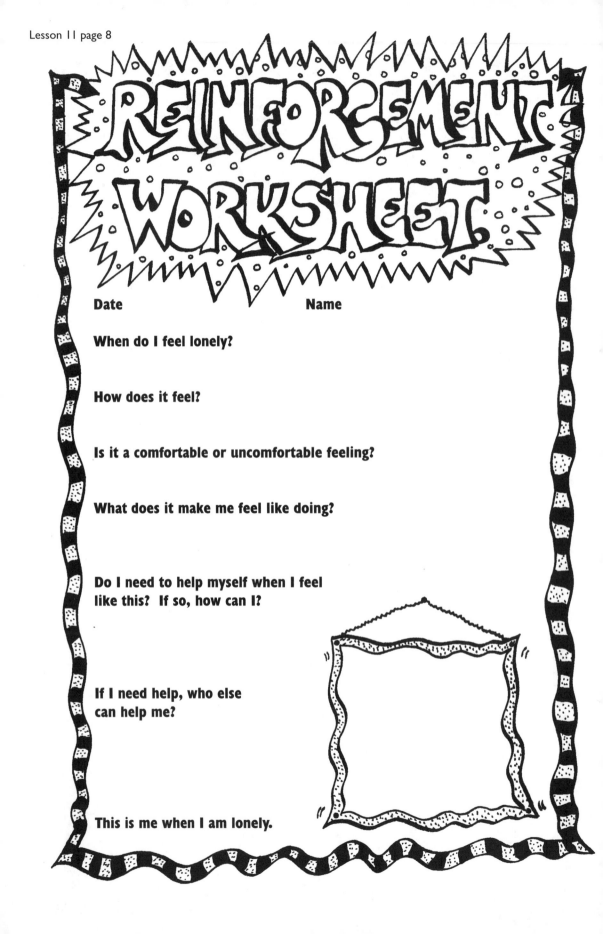

Lesson 12

Feeling Greedy

Definitions
is usually if you want too much of something and you eat or drink more than you really need.

Story 12 - Greedy

It was Christmas day. Alex and Sara crept down stairs on tip toes so as not to wake their mum.

"What time is it?" whispered Sara. Alex looked at the clock of the video.

"It's five to six," he said quietly, trying not to giggle as he dropped his stocking on the floor behind the big armchair.

"We can't open our presents yet - not until mum gets up and we'd better not wake her until at least seven - she'll go mad otherwise."

Sara smiled. They both knew that mum had been up until nearly 1 o'clock that morning trying to get all the last minute presents wrapped up and preparing the turkey for the posh dinner. They'd smelt the stuffing cooking at half past twelve as they'd pretended to be asleep. Of course, they'd hardly slept at all. How could anyone sleep knowing there were going to be so many treats over the next two days.

"Look at that!" said Sara as they crept over to the sideboard in the living room.

"Wow!" said Alex. "I've never seen so much stuff.

The sideboard had been covered in red and gold paper. On top of this were placed plates, trays and boxes of all kinds of sweets, special biscuits and chocolates. There were bowls of white chocolate snowmen, Maltesers, Belgian chocolates, butter biscuits, Brazil nuts, walnuts, peanuts, raisins covered in white chocolate and dates and satsumas.

"Well there's so much there - I think we could have some breakfast," said Sara. "No one will notice if we move bits around."

"Anyway, we can't go and make any breakfast yet - mum would hear us." Their mum's bedroom was just above the kitchen and, as they lived in a fairly new house, the walls were not very thick. Sound seemed to travel too easily in this house according to their mum.

They both giggled as they began to pick out some sweets. "I've always wanted a Christmas chocolate breakfast," said Alex. They both placed a table mat from the sideboard onto the carpet and proceeded to lay out the sweets on top of them so as not to make any marks or crumbs on the carpet.

"Mum must have been so busy," said Sara as she at her first chocolate snowman.

"This is smashing - the chocolate's so creamy," said Alex licking his lips.

They sat eating for a further ten minutes.

"I've had enough," said Sara. "Do you want these last bits Alex?"

"Okay." Alex tipped the rest of Sara's sweets into his lap.

"I think I'm going to switch the telly on without the sound," said Sara. "The cartoons will be on and mum won't hear if we don't laugh too loudly."

They watched Road Runner, Bugs Bunny and then Power Rangers for the next hour.

All the time, Alex kept eating - one chocolate after another. Sara looked at him.

"I think you should stop eating them now," she said.

"Why?" asked Alex. "I'm still hungry you know." He laughed. "And they are nice."

"I know," said Sara. "But remember mum will want us to have some breakfast when she gets up and Nan's coming round with loads of stuff for the dinner."

"Oh don't moan," said Alex. "You know that boys can always eat much more than girls."

He proceeded to help himself to another handful of chocolate covered peanuts. Just then they heard their mum coming down the stairs.

"Happy Christmas!" she shouted. Sara and Alex jumped up as she came into the room. She was holding two big pillow cases - each of them bursting with presents. "Happy Christmas mum," they both replied as they gave her big bear hugs.

"Come on! Open them all up," she said. They both started to pull the paper from the presents. Sara screamed with delight as she opened up a handmade jewellery box.

"Oh thanks mum - it's really lovely - just what I wanted".

Alex was quiet.

He tore the paper from his first present really slowly. He knew that he should feel really excited and he could hear Sara yelling away next to him but he just felt odd. He couldn't move quickly. It was as if he was doing everything in slow motion. He looked up to see his mum watching him closely.

"Are you okay love?" she asked.

But he wasn't - of course he wasn't. How could he be okay? He'd actually turned quite pale in the face. He ran from the room and headed straight upstairs towards the bathroom.

"What is it?" said mum.

"I think he ate too much chocolate," said Sara. Of course he had and of course he was sick - and not just once. It was a Christmas day he'd certainly never forget.

Questions for discussion

1   Why didn't the children open their presents when they first got up?

2   Do you think that they were quite tired? Why?

3   Why couldn't they make a 'real' breakfast?

4   How do you think Sara knew that she'd had enough to eat?

5   Was Alex right? Can boys eat more than girls?

6   How did Alex feel when he was opening his presents?

Act the Story

Act the story until you get to the STOP face. Try to make a better ending to the 'greedy' story. How could Alex have made himself stop eating?

Activities

Make up your own story about a greedy person or animal. You could use the worksheet about greedy Graziella. Try to show how being greedy might get you into an uncomfortable situation or some kind of trouble. it may mean that you lose your friends.

Stop Light
You would like to share your sweets with your friend but she never shares hers so you eat them all in secret when she is not there. You know this is greedy. Use the Traffic Light Method to come up with the best solution.

Draw two large pictures - a greedy character and a generous character. Use a cartoon style and invent your own animal characters. Then try to list all their various characteristics, e.g. one has lots of friends, one has very few friends.

Reinforcement

Complete the Reinforcement Worksheet for the feeling GREEDY.

THE STORY OF GREEDY GRAZIELLA

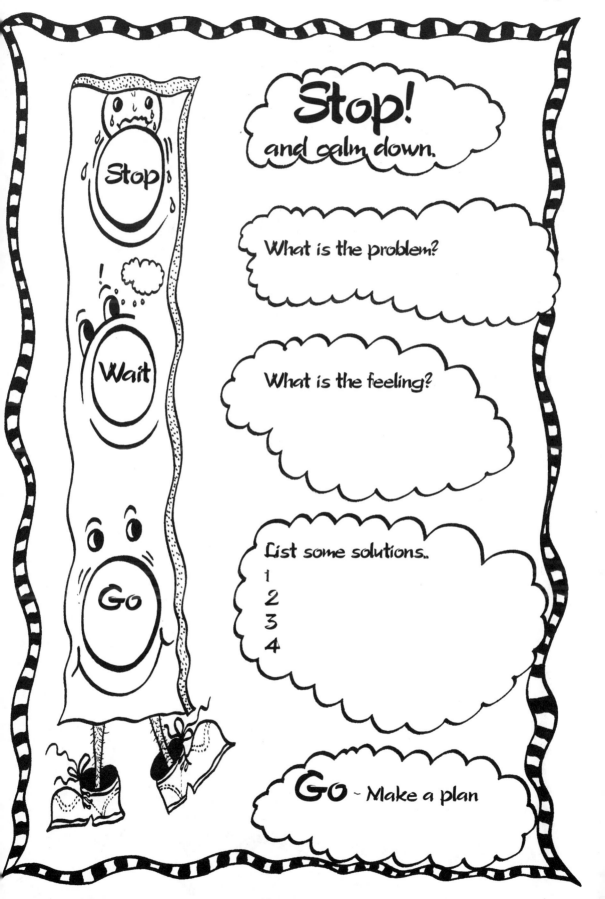

REINFORCEMENT WORKSHEET

Date   **Name**

When do I feel greedy?

How does it feel?

Is it a comfortable or uncomfortable feeling?

What does it make me feel like doing?

Do I need to help myself when I feel like this? If so, how can I?

If I need help, who else can help me?

This is me when I am greedy.

Lesson 13

Feeling Nervous

Definitions

is feeling fear & excitement
together. You may be afraid & jumpy.
It's not a very comfortable
feeling but it can be useful.

Story 13 - Nervous

Daniel jumped on his bike and pedalled as fast as he could to get to school by eight o'clock. His mum had shouted at him because he'd found it so hard to get out of bed.

But eight o'clock was really early, he thought as he arrived, panting, at the school hall. His Year 6 class had been busy rehearsing for almost two terms. They'd got a new teacher that year called Mr. Williams and he had been an actor before he became a teacher. Everyone really liked him. He was so funny and always told brilliant stories and acted the parts of each character. He made them laugh at least once every day and only seemed to get angry if people were being bullied or if they swore in front of him. Daniel liked him.

He had written the class a new version of the musical play ' Oliver' and they were due to perform it that Saturday night in the school hall. Mr. Williams had made it like a proper theatre company - all the kids had to audition. Dan had been quite nervous when he had been asked to act but he'd managed to sing really well. He had a good voice, so no one was surprised when Mr. Williams chose him to play Oliver.

No one except Dan's mum, that is. She laughed out loud.

"I don't know how you'll remember all those lines," she laughed.

Dan knew that she'd been joking but he couldn't help thinking about what she'd said.

I hope I remember it all, he thought as he locked the chain on his bike and went into the hall.

Mr. Williams was setting the blocks out on the stage.

"Hurry up Dan - get your costume on - it's our first full run today."

Dan gave him a weak smile.

"Are you okay?" asked Mr. Williams.

"Er ... yeah ... yep," said Dan and scuttled off to get changed.

But of course he wasn't okay. He met Hal and Caris backstage.

"How do you feel?" said Caris.

"Bad," said Dan. "I keep thinking I'm going to forget my lines."

"Me too," said Hal.

"Don't be daft," said Caris. "It's just nerves."

"Just nerves," said Hal. "JUST nerves!"

"Okay, okay, I know - but look, everyone feels like that. It'll be fine once we get out there and start the show."

Dan fiddled with his buttons. He couldn't get his hands to put them into the button holes. He was shaking.

"I know," he said. " .. it's just ... you know ... I ..."

Just then the house lights went up and the piano started. They were due in for the first number. Caris pulled Dan onto the stage behind her. It was the first time the lights had been used. Dan couldn't see a thing and it was so hot. He felt his face getting redder and redder. His throat felt dry and his head seemed to be pounding almost in time to the music. Just at that moment he heard his music. Caris pushed his elbow from behind and whispered "Go on Dan ... sing ... Go on!"

But he couldn't. He opened his mouth and nothing came out. He couldn't move. Caris nudged him again. He looked at her and mouthed "I can't." Then he ran off the stage as fast as he could possibly go.

Questions for discussion

1   Why did everyone like Mr. Williams?

2   Why was Daniel picked to play the part of Oliver?

3   Why had his mum made him feel so nervous?

4   What do you think Dan could have done to help himself?

5   What do you think Mr. Williams might have done if Daniel had been able to tell him how nervous he felt?

6   Do you think Caris was right when she said "It'll be fine when we start"?

7   Did Dan believe her?

8   How did Dan's nerves affect him physically? Give examples.

Act the Story

Act the story until you get to the STOP face.
Then work out a better ending for Dan.
Show how he overcomes this nervous feeling with the help of his teacher and friends.

Activities

Write a 'good ending' to the story. Describe how Daniel overcomes his nerves. He might even be spotted by a Talent Scout and become a famous star!

Think of ten things that make you feel nervous. Complete the illustrated list, e.g. the dentist, fast cars, spelling tests.

Stop Light

Janis is nervous about speaking out in front of other people. Everyone in her class has to give a five minute talk to the whole class about their favourite hobby. She feels she just can't do it. How can you help her? Make a 'best plan'.

Complete the Reinforcement Worksheet for the feeling NERVOUS.

Stop!
and calm down.

What is the problem?

What is the feeling?

List some solutions..
1
2
3
4

Go - Make a plan

Stop

Wait

Go

REINFORCEMENT WORKSHEET

Date   **Name**

When do I feel nervous?

How does it feel?

Is it a comfortable or uncomfortable feeling?

What does it make me feel like doing?

Do I need to help myself when I feel like this? If so, how can I?

If I need help, who else can help me?

This is me when I am nervous.

Lesson 14

Feeling Disappointed

Definitions

is when you feel let down. You may feel as if someone has failed or neglected you in some way. It's not a comfortable feeling.

Story 14 - Disappointed

The summer holidays seemed endless to Amy - mainly because all her friends had been away on holiday for the last two weeks and she'd been left on her own. Her mum had tried really hard to find her nice things to do but it was difficult. She had to go to work. For most of the day Amy had been on her own - 'entertaining herself', as Aunty Jermaine had put it.

The trouble is, thought Amy, I'm fed up with entertaining myself - I wish someone would just come along and take me somewhere exciting. I'm fed up with the Playcentre crowd. All the kids are much younger than me and the only ones of my age are boys. They're only happy if they're playing football. They're not interested in anything else.

She really felt fed up. Then the letter arrived. It was from Aunty Jermaine in Belgium.

Dear Amy

I know that you are bored - you certainly sounded bored when I phoned last Sunday. Why don't you come and stay with me for a couple of weeks? We can go to the Ardennes and stay in my Chalet. It will be great fun and there's lots for you to do there. Please ask your mum if it's okay and then I'll send you a ticket for the Hovercraft. We can pick you up in Ostende. Hope to see you soon.

Much love

Aunty Jermaine.

Amy was over the moon. She ran straight to her mum's shop.

"Look mum! It's from Aunty Jermaine. She says I can go and stay - isn't it great!"

"That'll be lovely for you," said her mum. "I know how fed up you've been this week. You'd better write back and say it's fine."

Amy gave her mum a kiss. "I'll go and write back now," she said.

She ran home, wrote a quick note saying that she'd love to come and took it down to the post office so that she could send it airmail.

"You look happy," said Miss Best from behind the counter.

"Well I am today," replied Amy, "because my Aunt's invited me to stay in Belgium for the holiday."

"Oh that sounds lovely - you lucky girl," said Miss Best, smiling.

Amy skipped out of the Post Office and down the road back to her house. She sat on the swing in the garden and thought about all the exciting things she would be able to do with her Aunty. She really loved her. She was such good fun and always seemed to be happy and laughing.

Well, I should get my tickets by Thursday at the latest. Miss Best said it takes two days each way if you go first class and it's Friday today, she thought.

The next Thursday morning she ran down to get the post. There was a gas bill and a catalogue for her mum - but no letter from Aunty Jermaine. She bit her lip.

"Never mind," said her mum. "It'll turn up tomorrow."

Amy went upstairs and sat on her bed with a book. She couldn't concentrate. She felt so upset. She had been so excited and now she just felt really let down.

Oh well, she thought. Maybe it's just the post - it may be slower than usual for some reason.

The next day she ran down to pick up the post again.

There was no letter. The same thing happened on Saturday. On Sunday morning Amy didn't feel like getting out of bed. She was utterly miserable. Her mum came upstairs with a cup of tea for her.

"Are you okay Amy?" she asked as she put the cup down on the table.

"Oh mum.." she began but she couldn't get any words out. She leant on her mum's arm and sobbed.

"There, there dear," said her mum. "I'm sure the letter will come. These things do take time."

"No, no ... it won't - I feel so upset mum. I thought that Aunty Jermaine really meant what she'd said in the letter. I thought she wanted me to go and stay and I was so looking forward to it ... m ... maybe she decided she didn't like me any more ...." She started to cry again.

"Now I'm sure that's not true," said her mum. "It must be something else."

Just then the door bell rang. Amy's mum ran downstairs to see who it was. She shouted upstairs. "Amy, Amy ... there's someone to see you."

Amy got out of bed, put on her dressing gown and went down the stairs.

"W ... w ... what! Aunty Jermaine!" she shouted. She ran down the stairs and gave both her Aunty and her mum the most enormous hug.

"Hello my darling," her Aunt said. "I decided not to write after all. I wanted to surprise you. I thought I'd come over to England and collect you so that we could go to the seaside here first - before we go to Belgium. I've never been to the English seaside. Where do you think we should go?"

Amy couldn't answer. She was laughing and crying at the same time.

I knew she wouldn't really let me down, she thought.

"Let's go into the kitchen and talk about it," said her mum. "I think we could all do with a nice cup of tea - don't you?"

Questions for discussion

1   Why was Amy so bored during the holidays?

2   Why didn't she want to play with the boys?

3   How did she feel when she received the letter from her Aunt?

4   What was so special about Aunty Jermaine?

5   How do you know that Amy felt disappointed when the letter didn't arrive? What clues are there in the story?

6   What feelings did Amy experience on Sunday morning as she spoke to her mum? How many can you think of?

7   Why do you think Amy was laughing and crying at the same time?

Act the Story

Show how Amy became more and more disappointed while she waited for the letter. Show how shocked she was when her Aunt finally arrived.

Activities

Write the next 'chapter' in this story. Where do they go? What do they do? The title could be - Amy's holiday adventure. Use these words : excited, thrilled, happy, loved, keen, generous, content, spoilt.

Make up your own cartoon story about someone who is disappointed. Use the activity sheet.

Stop Light

Sid worked hard to to learn his spellings but he only got four out of ten this week. His teacher made him learn them again in breaktime. Sid felt like giving up. He was very disappointed. Use the Traffic Light Method to come up with the best solution.

Reinforcement

Complete the Reinforcement Worksheet for DISAPPOINTED.

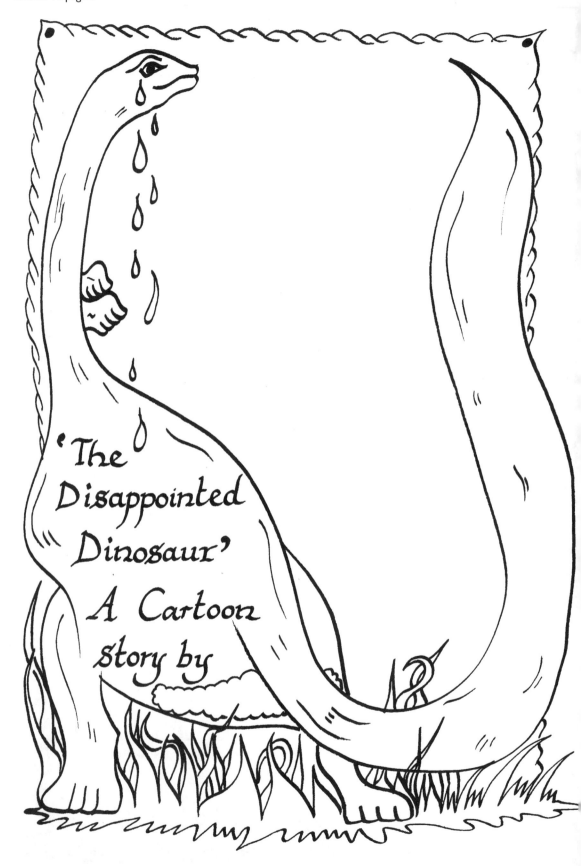

'The Disappointed Dinosaur'

A Cartoon story by

Stop!
and calm down.

What is the problem?

What is the feeling?

List some solutions..
1
2
3
4

Stop

Wait

Go

Go - Make a plan

REINFORCEMENT WORKSHEET

Date **Name**

When do I feel disappointed?

How does it feel?

Is it a comfortable or uncomfortable feeling?

What does it make me feel like doing?

Do I need to help myself when I feel like this? If so, how can I?

If I need help, who else can help me?

This is me when I am disappointed.

Lesson 15

Feeling Rejected

Definitions
is when you feel unloved, unwanted, pushed aside or excluded. It is a sad and uncomfortable feeling.

Story 15 - Rejected

Sally ran all the way to Jan's house. She stood panting in front of the door before she finally managed to reach up and touch the bell. Jan came to the door.

"Hi Sal. Come in, I'll just get my coat." Sally followed her into the hallway.

"We'd better hurry or we'll be late." she said. Jan shouted goodbye to her mum and took an orange from the fruit bowl in the kitchen.

"Oh, don't forget to tell Amy that you can go to her party on Saturday," said her mum.

"I won't," shouted Jan.

The two girls walked off down the street, sharing the orange as they went. It dribbled all over their coats and made their hands all sticky.

Sally sucked her fingers to try to get the sticky feeling to go away. She felt a bit funny. She hadn't said anything to Jan but she couldn't help it. There was a slight sick feeling in her stomach. Why had Jan been invited to Amy's party and she hadn't? What was wrong? She didn't understand it. After all, they all went round together - like a gang - her, Amy, Jan, Raff, Alex and Jake. Why was she being left out?

"You're quiet," said Jan. "Is everything okay?"

"Yep, fine," said Sally, as she gave a rather weak smile. But of course everything wasn't fine. She really felt like crying but she felt angry at the same time. She was determined not to show it though.

"Oh look! There's Amy and Raff," said Jan. She ran over to say hello.

"I can't wait until Saturday," said Amy.

"It'll be great," said Raff, turning to the two girls. "Amy's mum is paying for us to go ice-skating and to see the new 101 Dalmatians film."

"Brilliant," said Jan

Sally stood still and said nothing until Amy turned round and smiled at her.

"Are you okay Sal?" she asked. "You seem a bit quiet"

Sally looked at her. She bit her lip. She really wanted to ask her why she hadn't been invited - but she couldn't do it. She felt so hurt, angry and left out. She felt her face going red. It felt hot.

"Just go away!" she shouted. "You don't really like me anyway. You're just mean and stupid and I hate you." She ran off crying. The others stood still. They were so shocked.

"What on earth was all that about?" said Raff

"I don't know," said Amy. "it's just not like her at all."

"She was a bit funny this morning though - sort of quiet," said Jan.

"Well, we'll just have to go to school or we'll be late and get detentions," said Jake. Amy looked worried.

"Don't worry," said Jan. "We'll find her after school and get it sorted out."

Sally ran all the way home with tears streaming down her face. She knew her mum would be at work but she couldn't have cared less if anyone had caught her. She put the key in the door and went into the flat. As she looked down she saw the mail on the doormat and automatically picked it up and placed it on the telephone table. Then she suddenly looked back. There was a large pink envelope addressed to her. She opened it and read the first line - 'You are invited to Amy's birthday extravaganza'!' She stared down at the gold lettering. Tears fell and blurred the words.

Oh no! she thought. But it was too late now.

Questions for discussion

1 What sort of feeling did Sally have when she heard that Jan was invited to Amy's party?

2 Why do you think she lied to Jan and said she felt fine?

3 Why was Sally so determined to show that she wasn't upset?

4 Do you think she should have asked Amy about the party?

5 Do Sally's friends really care about her? If so, can you say how you know this?

6 How do you think Sally felt when she saw the invitation?

7 Is it too late or can she sort out this problem? How?

Act the Story

Act the story until you get to the STOP face. Try to show how rejected Sally felt. Does this show in her face and in the way she stands?

Then make up a better ending for her and the gang.

Activities

Re-write the story and create a 'good' ending.
Show how Sally overcomes her feeling of rejection.
Focus on what the characters would really say to each other in this situation.

Stop Light
Write down what she should do at each stage of the process. Think carefully about developing a 'best plan'. Work in pairs and discuss first.

When a new baby arrives in a family an older child might feel a bit rejected because the baby gets all the attention. Talk in small groups about this and discuss whether any of you have had this experience.

Write an acrostic poem using the activity sheet.

Reinforcement

Complete the reinforcement worksheet for REJECTION.

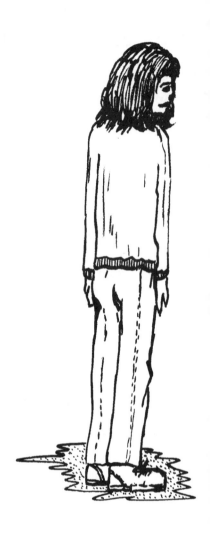

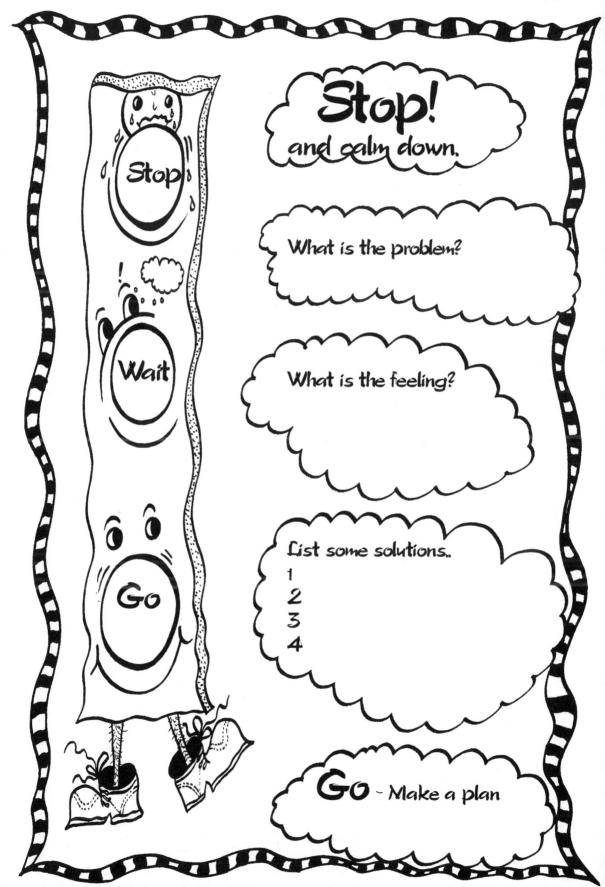

REINFORCEMENT WORKSHEET

Date   **Name**

When do I feel rejected?

How does it feel?

Is it a comfortable or uncomfortable feeling?

What does it make me feel like doing?

Do I need to help myself when I feel like this? If so, how can I?

If I need help, who else can help me?

This is me when I am rejected.

Lesson 16

Feeling Shy

Definitions

is when you are afraid of new people and situations. It's quite an uncomfortable feeling.

Story 16 - Shy

Barney wasn't looking forward to Monday. His family had moved from Scotland down to London during the summer because his dad had a new job in the Post Office. At first he'd been quite excited at the thought of moving to a new place - especially one that was the home of his favourite football team.

"Think of all the matches we can go to, instead of just watching them on the telly," said his dad.

Barney had thought quite a lot about that. Yep - it would be really great, he thought, but if he was really honest he still felt a bit scared about meeting a whole new crowd, starting a new school and getting used to the way that people talked in England. It was funny - he'd never really thought about the differences before but when he watched Eastenders on the telly now he wondered how they would understand him at school - after all, the accents were so different.

They packed and prepared for what seemed like weeks, and finally arrived on the Sunday night. He was due to start at Mayford Primary the next morning. It was all he thought about that night.

Will they like me? Will I be able to make friends?

When he got out of bed he felt that he hadn't actually slept a wink. His mum went with him to school where they met the Headteacher who then took them along to introduce him to his new class. The school looked much bigger than Ladywell in Glasgow and there seemed to be so many children.

"Chin up son," whispered his mum, as they walked up to the door. "It'll be fine - you'll soon make new friends."

He tried to smile but he felt sick inside. The class teacher came to the door and introduced herself.

"Hello Barney - I'm Mrs. Maconville," she said, smiling, as she held out her hand. She was tall and pretty and best of all she sounded Scottish!

Barney smiled.

At least she'll understand me, he thought. She introduced him to the class and showed him to his seat. He looked around the table. There were three boys and two girls. They all smiled at him and said hello. He tried to smile back but he felt too nervous and looked down at the table.

"Okay children - today we're starting our project on the Greeks - now, who can tell me anything about the Greek civilisation? Hands up please!"

Barney sat rigid in his seat. He knew tons about the Greeks. It had been his last project in school but he couldn't say anything. Other children talked about their Greek holidays and gave the names of Greek gods they knew from stories they had heard. Barney didn't say a word. He just looked at the table. Then he overheard the other children whispering.

"Gosh - he's quiet," said Alex, who was sitting opposite him.

"Perhaps he's nervous - it must be hard starting a new school," said Caris and she smiled across at Barney encouragingly. He didn't smile back. He couldn't. He was beginning to feel really miserable.

Then the bell went for play.

"Alex, can you take Barney to the playground with you please?" said Mrs. Maconville. "He'll need to know where the toilets are as well."

"Yes Miss." said Alex, and he beckoned Barney to follow him.

"Where are you from?" asked Alex.

Barney managed to say, "Scotland."

"Oh - it's lovely there, isn't it?" said Caris.

"Yeah - all the mountains and stuff," said Jos.

Barney looked at his feet. He really wanted to chat to them. They seemed so kind and were really trying to make friends with him. But he just couldn't open his mouth and get the words out.

"Are you okay?" said Caris.

Barney didn't speak. Just then Sam came across the playground with his football.

"Do you want a game?" he asked.

"Great," said Caris. "Come on Barney - do you want to play?"

Barney was brilliant at football and he would have loved to play a game, but again - he felt so nervous that he didn't reply.

"Well, we're going to play - we'll get you when the bell goes," she said.

Barney stood on his own, watching they as they ran off to the pitch.

"I think he's just a snob," said Jos.

"Yeah - he must be," said Alex, "otherwise he'd have played a game."

"I don't know," said Caris, "maybe he's just shy."

"Oh don't be soft," said Alex. " He won't even look us in the face. He thinks that he's better than us and that's why he won't play. Forget him."

"Yeah - we don't want him in our gang anyway," said Jos.

Poor Barney - he could hear what they were saying. He felt worse than ever now. I just wish I wasn't so shy, he thought.

He wasn't a snob - he knew that for a fact. But how was he going to show them now?

Maybe it was too late already.

Questions for discussion

1   Why was Barney so nervous about starting his new school?

2   What could he have done to help himself?

3   What do you think he should have said to Caris?

4   What do you think Barney felt like at the end of play?

5   What do you think will happen next?

6   Have you ever felt shy? When? Why? What happened?

Act the Story

Act the story until you get to the STOP face. Try to work out a better ending for Barney.

Activities

Can you remember your first day at school, or at a new school? Did you feel excited, nervous or shy?

Write a letter to a good friend and describe your first day to them. If you can't remember your first day then try to imagine that you are Barney. Write a letter from him to a friend back in Scotland. Describe the events of the day and his feelings.

Stop Light
Barney needs a better ending! Use the traffic light method to work out a way for him to deal with his feelings of shyness.

Work out five ways to stop being SHY' Work with a friend. Use the activity sheet to solve Fred's problem. Write him a letter.

Reinforcement

Complete the Reinforcement Worksheet for the feeling SHY.

FRED is SHY

Can you help him? Write him a letter.

Dear Fred,

Stop!
and calm down.

What is the problem?

What is the feeling?

List some solutions..
1
2
3
4

Go - Make a plan

Stop

Wait

Go

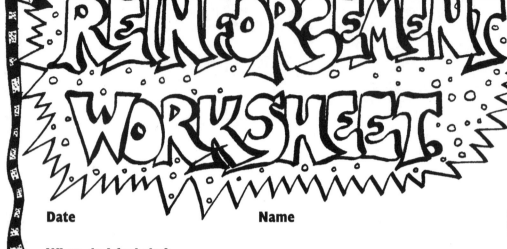

REINFORCEMENT WORKSHEET

Date   **Name**

When do I feel shy?

How does it feel?

Is it a comfortable or uncomfortable feeling?

What does it make me feel like doing?

Do I need to help myself when I feel like this? If so, how can I?

If I need help, who else can help me?

This is me when I am shy.

Lesson 17

Feeling Arrogant

Definitions

is when you think too much of yourself. You are the "best" and feel arrogant and look down on others.

Story 17 - Arrogant

Anna woke up as the alarm clock buzzed at 7 am. She yawned and turned over.

Just five more minutes, she thought. She was so cosy and warm in bed and she knew that it was really cold because the windows were covered in frost on the inside and her breath made a white cloud as she breathed out. She shivered and tucked the duvet around her shoulders.

"Anna! Anna! Come on. It's time to get up - hurry up. Don't you remember what day it is?" shouted her mum from the kitchen.

"No - she's too daft, not with it," shouted her brother Sam from the bathroom. Anna jumped.

Oh no! she thought. I slept so well and dreamt so much - it just went out of my head. She jumped out of bed and ran to the bathroom.

"Come on Sam - hurry up! I've got the ice-skating competition today - hurry up or else I'll be late!"

He poked his head round the door and smiled.

"I know," he said and ruffled her hair as he ran past. Anna ran in and put the shower on. She looked in the mirror and smiled.

I know I'm going to win, she thought. After all, I'm the best skater and I look the best.

She tied up her long hair and jumped into the shower.

An hour and a half later she was sitting at the side of the ice rink. Mum had made her a new outfit just for this competition. It was really lovely - all red velvet trimmed with white fur. It had gold sequins sewn onto the skirt and gold brocade around the edges of the neck and sleeves.

"You look really nice," said Sara as she sat down in her place next to Anna.

"Thanks," said Anna. She looked at Sara's outfit and thought, Well, I can't say the same for you - pity!

"I'm nervous," said Sara. "Aren't you?"

"No - not really," said Anna. "I'm more.... well, excited. After all, there isn't anything to be nervous about, not if you've practised as much as I have. I've done five hours a day for the last three weeks and my routine's really excellent now." She smiled at Sara. Sara was quiet. She looked down at her boots.

I wish I was confident like her - it must be nice. I just can't help it. I feel so nervous, she thought. Number 72 was then relayed over the loudspeaker system.

"Go on! That's you!" said Anna. Sara jumped up. She took a deep breath and started to move onto the ice. She counted to ten and held out her arms as her music began. She concentrated as hard as she could and tried to remember everything her teacher had told her to do - stay calm, think, move carefully and slowly and concentrate! She finished her routine and took her bow. The audience were still clapping as she sat down next to Anna. She was out of breath and pink in the face.

"Whew! I'm glad that's over," she said.

"Ssh!" hissed Anna. Listen - it's your results."

The number came over the loud speaker system:

| 5.4 | 5.6 | 5.7 | 5.3 | 5.6 | 5.7 |

"Um - not bad," said Anna smiling.

"Thanks," said Sara. She was really pleased. "I hadn't expected to do that well! Oh! That's your number Anna - Good Luck!"

Anna stood up.

"It's nothing to do with luck," she said as she skated smoothly onto the ice. Her music began and she started her routine.

She looks so confident, thought Sara. I bet she wins.

Just then Anna went for her big jump but as she span round she caught her blade in the bottom of her skirt and missed her footing. She landed with a big thump on the ice - on her bottom! There was a hush in the ice rink as people waited to see what she would do. She stood up and tried the move again, but the same thing happened - she fell and this time she skidded from the middle of the rink right to the side where the judges were sitting. Her face was bright red.

"She looks furious," said Sara to Caris.

"I bet she is," said Caris. "And look at those scores!"

The judges read out:

| 4.8 | 4.6 | 4.7 | 4.3 | 4.6 | 4.7 |

Anna stormed off the ice and walked straight past the two girls. She went through to the dressing room without uttering a word to anyone. Tears were burning her cheeks.

"Oh no! What a shame," said Sara.

"Not really," said Caris. "She might learn her lesson now - as my Gran always used to say, "'Pride comes before a fall'.""

Questions for discussion

1   Do you think Anna felt nervous about the ice skating competition?
    What clues does the story give you?

2   How did she know that she was going to win?

3   Why was Sara nervous?

4   Why do you think that Sara skated well? What did she do to help
    herself?

5   What did Anna mean when she said "It's nothing to do with luck"?

6   What do you think Caris meant when she said "Pride comes before a
    fall"?

7   What do you think Anna will do next? Do you think that she might
    have learnt a lesson?

Act the Story

Try to show how different characters felt - how nervous Sara was and how
arrogantly Anna felt and acted. Show the relief on Sara's face and in her
voice when she completes her routine well. Think about how upset Anna
will feel at the end of her routine. What will happen next?

Activities

Make up your own story entitled 'Pride comes before a fall'. At the start
of the story you will need to introduce your main character very carefully
and describe the arrogant manners and behaviour.
    What happens?
    How does he or she 'fall'?
    Does he or she learn a real lesson?
    Use the activity sheet.

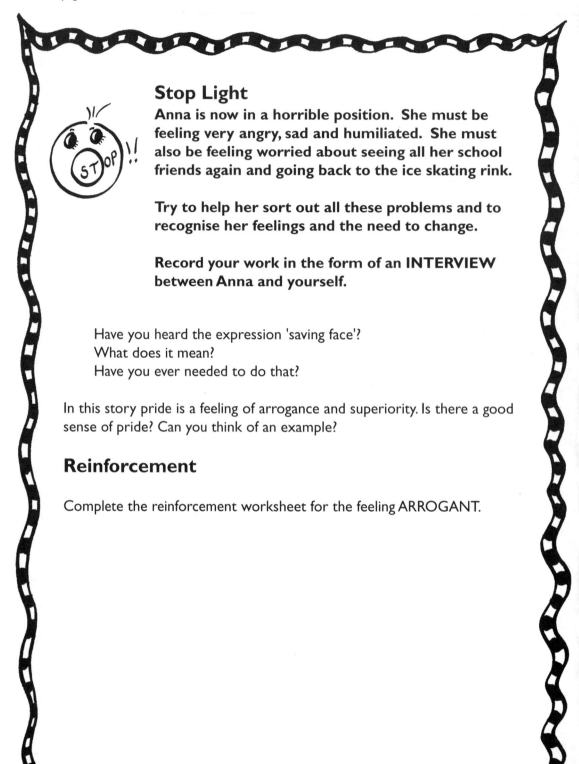

Stop Light

Anna is now in a horrible position. She must be feeling very angry, sad and humiliated. She must also be feeling worried about seeing all her school friends again and going back to the ice skating rink.

Try to help her sort out all these problems and to recognise her feelings and the need to change.

Record your work in the form of an **INTERVIEW** between Anna and yourself.

Have you heard the expression 'saving face'?
What does it mean?
Have you ever needed to do that?

In this story pride is a feeling of arrogance and superiority. Is there a good sense of pride? Can you think of an example?

Reinforcement

Complete the reinforcement worksheet for the feeling ARROGANT.

REINFORCEMENT WORKSHEET

Date   **Name**

When do I feel arrogant?

How does it feel?

Is it a comfortable or uncomfortable feeling?

What does it make me feel like doing?

Do I need to help myself when I feel like this? If so, how can I?

If I need help, who else can help me?

This is me when I am arrogant.

Lesson 18

Feeling Generous

Definitions

is when you really share
your self and your possessions
with others.

Story 18 - Generous

Hal and Janet ran home and almost fell into their house through the patio window. Hal certainly might have fallen right through the window if his dad hadn't been standing there re-potting his spider plants.

"Wow! Hold on son! What's the big rush?" he said as Hal's head hit his right arm.

"Ooops! Sorry dad - it's just, well - we're so excited."

"I can see that," said his dad.

Hal continued ".. because we've been invited to Sid's party and it's bound to be brilliant!"

"Yeah - like last year - it went on for hours," said Janet, "and we got brilliant presents."

"Right! What's all the fuss about?" said mum as she came in from mowing the lawn. "I could hear you two half way down the garden."

"It's Sid's party," laughed dad.

"Oh no! not that again - I suppose we'll have to put up with you being spoilt rotten for another whole weekend."

"But mum," said Janet, "it is only once a year and it is the best party we ever get to go to."

"It must cost Sid's parents an absolute fortune - what is it this year?"

"It's a Disney theme," said Janet laughing.

"Ah well! I suppose that means you'll all be off to Disney Land - ha! ha! ha!" laughed dad.

Janet and Hal laughed and ran upstairs to look through the clothes in the dressing up box. Mum shut the patio doors.

"You know," she said. "I know Sid's dad is rich, but he really shouldn't spend all this money on everyone else's kids."

"Why on earth not?" said dad. "After all, they've got the money to do it and it certainly makes all the children happy - I think it's great."

"Well - you would," she said. "You're nothing more than a kid yourself." Dad laughed.

The next day the invitation came through the letter box. It read:

Hal and Janet

You are invited to Sid's 10th birthday party. You will need a Disney costume and a passport plus permission from your mum and dad to spend a week in Florida.

We hope you can come

Love from Sid, Ella and Joe

P T O

Janet and Hal screamed with excitement when they read the invitation.

"It's like a dream come true," said Hal. "I've always wanted to go to America."

"And Disney Land - it'll be brilliant!" said Janet.

Dad took the invitation from Hal and read it through again. "It's true - that's where you are going you lucky things! I wish I was coming too." He sighed.

"Hold on dad - look! is says PTO on the right hand corner of the card - what does that mean?"

"Please turn over," said mum laughing.

Dad read aloud:

"P S mums and dads are invited too - let's all have a holiday!"

"I don't believe it," said mum. "I know they're rich - but this is just so generous - do you think we should?"

"No question about it," said dad. "We're all going and that's that. Ella and Joe know what they're doing. They've got the money to do it and they want to do it for all of us. It's great and I can't wait," he said. Everyone laughed out loud except mum who suddenly seemed a bit withdrawn.

"What is it love?" asked dad.

"I don't know," she said. "It's just - well, we could never afford to do this for our own kids let alone all the families in the street."

"No we couldn't," replied dad. "But then we didn't win a lot of money on the lottery. What you've got to remember is this - Joe and Ella were always kind and generous when they had no money at all. We should just be glad that having money hasn't made them mean. They've stayed just the same and it's the way they want to be. I'm glad. That's all I can say."

"And so are we," said Hal and Janet.

Mum smiled. "Me too!" she said. "But I'm going to insist on paying for the first round of mega-cokes and ice-cream - and that's final!"

Questions for discussion

1 Why were Janet and Hal so excited?

2 Do you think dad really thought the children would be going to Disney Land or did he just make a joke?

3 Did mum feel happy with the idea of Sid's parents paying for everything?

4 Why did dad feel they could accept the generous offer?

5 Where had Ella and Joe got all their money from?

6 What sort of people had they been before their big win?

7 Has anyone ever been really generous towards you? Where? Why? What happened?

8 Have you ever been really generous towards a friend or a member of your family? Where? Why? What did you do?

Act the story

Show the excitement that the whole family felt in this story. You may want to make up an ending or show the family staying in Florida and making their visit to Disney Land.

Activities

Ask you teacher to read 'The Selfish Giant' to the class. This story is by Oscar Wilde. Think about the changes that take place in this story - particularly for the Giant. His life is changed beyond recognition. Make up your own story called 'The Generous Giant' and show how the personality of this giant changes others who are mean and selfish.

Make up an Acrostic Poem making use of the word: GENEROSITY.

Try to think of as many things as possible that could be seen as generous - things that you might do to help others, acts of kindness or sharing. e.g. giving presents, giving love, sharing games and time, running to the shop for Gran, etc.

Use the activity sheet for your list.

Reinforcement

Complete the Reinforcement Worksheet for the feeling GENEROUS.

REINFORCEMENT WORKSHEET

Date   **Name**

When do I feel generous?

How does it feel?

Is it a comfortable or uncomfortable feeling?

What does it make me feel like doing?

Do I need to help myself when I feel like this?

This is me when I am generous.

Lesson 19

Feeling Selfish.

Definitions
is when you only think of
yourself and don't care about the
needs and feelings of others.

Story 19 - Selfish

It was only one week until Christmas and there were only three more school days left before they broke up for the holidays. Anna was really excited. She'd written a list of 12 things for her mum and dad to get her and left it on her mum's bedside table. She knew that both her parents couldn't have missed it because she wrote it on an enormous piece of paper.

She'd asked for a new computer, two dresses, a make-up box, a pair of ice skates, some Nike trainers, twenty two CDs, an Encyclopaedia, a personal stereo, a pair of gold earrings and a matching bracelet.

Maybe I should have asked for a new leather bag as well, she thought as she walked to school for the Christmas party.

Still, I can always add that to the list later.

As she walked along, she clutched her bag of chocolate angels. Her mum had given them to her to hand round at the Christmas party, but she'd eaten four of them already.

Um, they are lovely, she thought as she unwrapped another one and popped it in her mouth.

The party was lovely - there was so much food to eat and they played some really good games. Pass the Parcel was the best. Anna managed to grab hold of the parcel twice at the last moment and ripped off enough paper to win both prizes. She also won three quiz games because she was so quick at answering questions.

"It's not fair," said Alex to Sam. "She's won five prizes - I haven't got anything yet."

Miss Best overheard.

"Never mind," she said. "I've got a special present for all of you at the end of the party. Everyone will be a winner then."

She smiled at Alex and Sam. She was very kind and obviously wanted all the children in her class to enjoy the party on the last day of term. Anna stared at the two boys and then looked down at the pile of gifts she had won. The plastic bag containing the chocolate angels was half empty as she'd eaten so many of them.

I suppose I could give Alex the playing cards, she thought. I won't play with them myself - I don't like cards much.

She picked up the cards but then thought again.

Well ... I did win them - he didn't - why should he have them just because he's too stupid to win any prizes. She put the cards back into her carrier bag and tied up the top handles.

I don't want anyone taking my things, she thought.

At the end of the party they played musical bumps. Anna was very careful not to move around too much so that, at the end of the game, she was in the last two with Caris. Caris hadn't won a prize, but it was almost as if she was trying too hard to win the game. She tripped over and got up just as they music game came to a stop. Anna had managed to get down on the carpet first.

Great! another prize for me! she thought.

"Well done!" said Miss Best - but she wasn't smiling.

At the end of the party everyone helped to clear up including some of the parents who had come to help. Alex and Jake ran to Jake's mum as she came to the door. "Have you got my invitations?" said Jake "did you write them for me?"

His mum laughed. "Of course I did - here you go - you'd better hand them out before all the kids go home."

"What is it?" said Caris.

"Well, it's my birthday on Christmas Eve and, because it's the holidays, I've never been able to have a proper party. Anyway, mum's organised a brilliant treat for the whole class - we're going on a coach, all of us - to Maxton's Theme Park. Then we're going to a movie and finishing up with pizzas."

"That sounds brilliant," said Alex.

"It's really kind of your mum - she's very generous," said Caris laughing.

They ran round the room and made sure everyone had an invitation. There were screams of delight as the invitations were opened. It seemed like Christmas was just one treat after another and this one sounded really great - the best yet.

Anna waited for her invitation. She waited right until the very end when the cleaning up had been finished, but by then Alex, Jake and Caris had gone home. So had everyone else. She stood looking at her bag of chocolate angels - there were only three left.

"Is your mum picking you up or are you going home on your own this afternoon?" asked Miss Best as she picked up the last of the party poppers.

"Oh - um ... on my own," said Anna.

"Well - be careful, and have a lovely holiday," said Miss Best.

"Thanks Miss," she said as she walked out of the room. She walked slowly up the hill. Actually, she felt a bit sick from having eaten too much chocolate and also she felt quite annoyed. Why didn't I get an invitation to Jake's party? It's not fair. Everyone else did. Why didn't I?

Perhaps we know the answer - or do we?

Questions for discussion

1   Why was Anna so excited at the start of the story?

2   Do you think that she was right to eat the chocolate angels as she walked to school?

3   How was Miss Best going to 'make it fair' for all the children in her class?

4   What could Anna have done with the playing cards?

5   Why do you think that Miss Best didn't smile when she said "Well done" to Anna after the musical bumps game?

6   Why did Caris think Jake's mum was generous?

7   How did Anna feel when she didn't get an invitation?

8   Why do you think that Jake didn't want her at his party?

9   Do you think Anna will be able to really make friends? If not, why not? What do you think she'd have to do in order to have friends at school?

Act the Story

Act the story until you get to the STOP face. Then try to make up a better ending for Anna. Can you show how she changes from being selfish to being kind and thinking about the other children in her class.

Activities

Write a better ending to the 'Selfish Story' Start at the STOP face and change Anna's actions so that she does the 'right' thing and, in the end, receives an invitation to Jake's party.

Christmas is traditionally a time for giving and sharing. Make a list of your friends. What would you like to give them and why? Think about their needs and likes. e.g. Mum - a new necklace - because her old one broke and she lost little bits of it. She's always wanted a new one. Jan - a bunch of flowers as she loves them and she hasn't got a garden.

Work in pairs and complete the activity sheet.
Lead in to this activity with a discussion about:
    How people can avoid being selfish?
    What are the benefits?

Reinforcement

Complete the reinforcement worksheet for SELFISH.

REINFORCEMENT WORKSHEET

Date **Name**

When do I feel selfish?

How does it feel?

Is it a comfortable or uncomfortable feeling?

What does it make me feel like doing?

Do I need to help myself when I feel like this? If so, how can I?

If I need help, who else can help me?

This is me when I am selfish.

Lesson 20

Feeling Intimidated

Definitions
is when you feel afraid of a person or a group. You may be bullied or frightened into doing something you don't want to do.

Story 20 - Intimidated

Sam got out of the car and waved to his mum. As he watched her drive around the corner he felt sick. There was nothing he could do about it. He would just have to go into the playground and face it. He took a deep breath and walked slowly through the gates. As he got to A Block he saw them waiting. Jos Deacon .... he hated that name - but there he was, standing large as life in front of him.

"Where do you think you're going then?" Jos asked.

He stood in front of Sam, preventing him from walking any nearer to the school buildings.

"Into class .... where else?" Sam replied.

"Oh - who's a rude boy then?" said Daniel.

He pushed Sam hard and nearly made him fall over.

"He's going red - look!"

The gang all laughed.

I mustn't cry, thought Sam. I mustn't.

He took a deep breath and tried to keep calm.

"What have you got for us today then?" asked Jos. "It had better be good - we're short of money at the moment - a fiver should do it."

"But I haven't got a fiver. My mum only gave me two pounds today - it's for my lunch."

"Right then - hand it over," hissed Mike.

"Yeah - or else we'll do you right now," said Jos.

Just then Mr. Jeffers walked past. He stopped and looked back at the group "Everything okay boys?" he said. Sam looked at his feet.

"Yeah, fine Mr. Jeffers - we're just going into class," said Jos.

"Well, hurry up then - you don't want late marks," he said.

He turned away from them and walked briskly across the playground. The boys crowded around Sam. "Well come on then you fat chicken - hand it over." Sam didn't move. He couldn't. He was just too scared.

"Oh dear, oh dear," said Jos in his creepy voice. "He doesn't want to play today."

"Oh dear, oh dear. We'll just have to MAKE him," said Mike. He grabbed Sam's hair on the back of his head and pulled it hard. Daniel kicked him in the leg while Jos grabbed his bag. He emptied it's contents onto the ground. Two one pound coins fell out on top of the homework book.

"What a creep you are! Look, you lot - two pounds, that's all," said Mike.

"Not enough you know - you'd better bring some more tomorrow - right!"

Sam just looked at them. Daniel picked up the homework book.

"Look you lot! The fat chicken has done his homework." He opened the book and looked at it.

"Give it back," said Sam in a quiet voice. He was shaking.

"You'll have to come and get it," said Daniel. "You'll have to come and get it from the toilets - that's where it'll be." With that, the boys ran off, tearing pages out of his book as they went. All Sam could hear was their laughter. It just didn't seem to stop.

Questions for discussion

1   Why did Sam feel so sick when his mum left?

2   What did the boys want from Sam?

3   Do you think he'd given them money before this? Why?

4   What did Jos mean when he said "We'll do you"? What do you think they intended to do if Sam hadn't given them the money?

5   Do you think that the teacher knew what was happening?

6   What could Sam have done to help himself?

7   What do you think will happen next?

Act the Story

Act the story until you get to the STOP face. Try to work out a better ending for Sam.

Activities

Write a good ending to the story from the STOP face.

Stop Light
Pretend you are one of Sam's class mates and you know what is happening to him. Write down how you feel about bullying. Then make an ACTION PLAN which will help you to sort out the problem. Follow the traffic Light Method to develop your best plan.

Working in a group discuss your answers to these questions.
1 What makes a bully behave in this way?
2 Does he or she often need to act big in front of a group?
3 How does a bully look?
4 How does a bully feel?
5 Are bullies always strong or are they sometimes sad or worried
   or jealous?

How can we stop bullying in schools? Think of four ways that might
work. Discuss it with a partner. Use the activity sheet to help you
develop your ideas.

Reinforcement

Complete the reinforcement worksheet for INTIMIDATION.

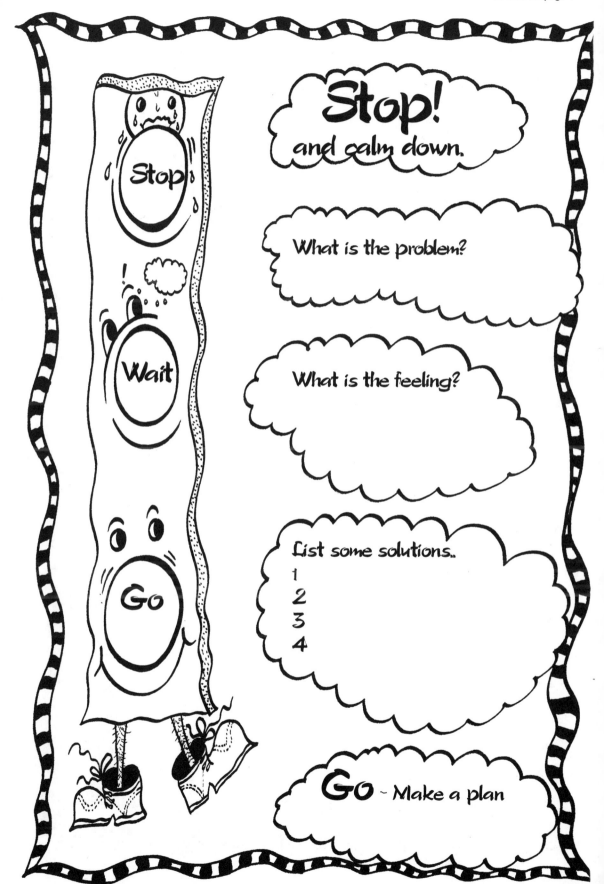

REINFORCEMENT WORKSHEET

Date   **Name**

When do I feel intimidated?

How does it feel?

Is it a comfortable or uncomfortable feeling?

What does it make me feel like doing?

Do I need to help myself when I feel like this? If so, how can I?

If I need help, who else can help me?

This is me when I am intimidated.

More Resources

a cover for a feelings book
brainstorming / recording worksheets
3 problem solve worksheets
32 problems to solve.

We decided on this solution.

The problem is

Remember

Stop..

Think..

Say!

These problems can be solved in groups or by brainstorming in whole class situations or by pupils working individually.

The problems have been formulated by both staff and children who have worked on the Emotional Awareness Training Programme.

They are problems that pupils themselves have experienced or encountered in their daily lives.

Remember

◆   You can use the Problem Solve Worksheet.

◆   You can use the Traffic Light Method.

◆   You can imagine that the problem is your own.

◆   You can make up your own problem.

◆   You can problem solve a real problem of your own or a problem that your friend has.

Problem Solving Worksheet

The problem is:

Think - What is wrong? Say it to yourself clearly.

Say:

What can I do? Think of as many solutions as you can.

Choose your best plan. Think of as many reasons why this might work for you.

I chose plan

What will be better now?

Why do you think this?

Okay - try it out!

Signed   Date

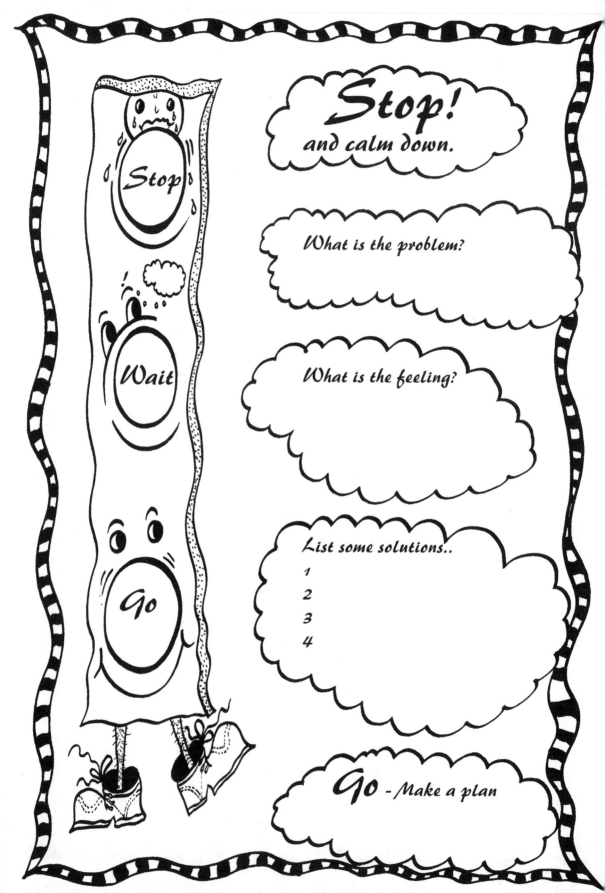

Problems to Solve

1   Someone is cussing your mum in the playground. They have been doing this for three weeks and you are feeling fed up.

   What can you do?

2   Your friend's mum and dad have split up. She is very sad about this and has started to take it out on you by losing her temper and sulking.

   What can you do?

3   Jake wasn't picked for the school football team. He feels that he should have been picked and is angry with his teacher.

   What can he do?

4   You have to start a new school. You feel very nervous.

   What can you do to help yourself?

5   Your friend is always getting new things because her mum and dad have plenty of money. You feel jealous because your mum can't afford to buy you new things very often.

   What can you do?

6   Your dad has left home because he doesn't want to live with your mum any more. Your mum promised that you could go and stay with him at weekends in his new flat, but now she says that she doesn't want you to have anything to do with him.

   What can you do?

7   Your friend has been picked to be the star part in the school play. She has become very big-headed and has been boasting about how good she is in the play. People are saying that they don't like her anymore and that she is a show-off.

   What can you do?

8   You don't like your next door neighbour because he keeps telling lies about you to your mum. Yesterday he said that you smashed his window with your football. You know it wasn't you because you saw Jake kick the ball at his house. You feel hurt and angry.

   What can you do?

9   You are fat and people in school keep teasing you about it. They have been really horrible to you and now you feel sick every day and don't want to go to school.

   What can you do?

10   Your mum has got a new job and she's not home until 6pm. You miss her as there's no one else around to talk to when you get in from school.

   What can you do?

11   Two boys in your class keep tripping people up on their way to assembly. Last week they really hurt one girl, but the teachers didn't see and she's too scared to tell anyone.

   What can you do?

12   Your best friend has gone to live in India. You are quite shy and will really miss him.

   What can you do?

13   You are feeling fed up and don't want to go to school because you can't read very well. People have been calling you a dummy - especially in class where you find the work too hard.

   What can you do?

14   Your best friend is on holiday and you are lonely. Your other friends don't want to play with you and you feel bored.

   What can you do?

15   A new girl comes into your class. She is from Kenya. People tease her because she's black and speaks English with a different accent. You feel very uncomfortable about this.

   What can you do?

16   Your mum is paying so much attention to your new baby brother, she doesn't have any time for you. You feel jealous and hurt.

   What can you do?

17   You have been made the goalkeeper in your class football team. Sam and Jon have said that if you let any goals in then they will beat you up after school. You feel sick and frightened of them.

   What can you do?

18   You mum and dad keep arguing and last night your dad shouted really loud and hit your mum. You feel worried, sad and upset.

What can you do?

19   Your friend stole your football and now he says that it is his and that his dad bought it for him. You feel angry about this and hurt because he's never done anything like this before.

What can you do?

20   A Year 6 boy keeps swearing at you when you go out to play at break times. You tell the teacher and then everyone gangs up on you.

What can you do?

21   You are jealous of your little sister. Your mum and dad keep buying her things - especially games and toys and they haven't given you anything new for months. You feel so angry with them and you just want to hit her.

What can you do?

22   Everyone in your class is getting new trainers. You dad can't afford to buy you a pair. Some of the kids in your class are saying that you're a tramp be-cause you have to wear old trainers.

What can you do?

23   Your nan died and you really miss her. You feel sad and can't concentrate in lessons. The teacher said that you were lazy. This embarrassed you in front of the whole class. She didn't know about your nan.

What can you do?

24   Carla has been away from school and staying with her aunt in Spain. She hasn't spoken English for the whole year and she's really worried that she's forgotten how to and that people in school will tease her.

   What can she do?

25   Jake just can't catch the ball or throw it properly. Sports Day is coming up again and he's feeling really nervous because he knows that no-one will want him on their team as they'll get fed up with him not getting any points.

   What can he do?

26   Mr. Morgan 'swops' with your teacher on Wednesday mornings. She takes his class for music and he takes you for a mental maths session. He shouts at your because you can't do the work.

   What can you do?

27   A new boy has come into your class and your friend really likes him and has invited him round to watch a video on Friday night, but you haven't been invited. You feel left out.

   What can you do?

28   You just can't learn spellings. You feel really frustrated because they don't seem to 'stick' in your head. Everyone else seems to find them easy, but you don't. There is a test every week and you only got 2 out of 20 last time.

   What can you do?

29   You hate going to the swimming pool every Thursday because the teachers make you put your face in the water. You are really frightened, but also too scared to tell anyone in case they think that you're a wimp.

What can you do?

30   The teacher keeps picking on you and telling you off - even when you don't do anything wrong.

What can you do?

31   Two girls in your class went into the room at break time and took £5 from the teacher's drawer. You saw them do this through the window. They saw you and said that they'd beat you up after school if you told anyone. You feel scared.

What can you do?

32   You haven't done your homework and this is the fourth time that this has happened. Your teacher will be angry.

What can you do?

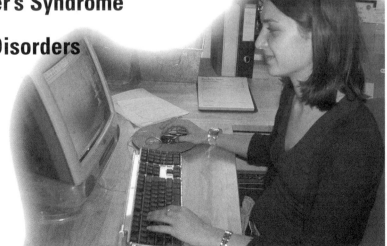